message:send

Communicating the Gospel
in a Post-Truth Culture

John Peters

RIVER
PUBLISHING

River Publishing & Media Ltd
Bradbourne Stables
East Malling
Kent ME19 6DZ
United Kingdom

info@river-publishing.co.uk

Published in partnership with New Wine Trust

www.new-wine.org

ISBN 978-1-908393-67-8
Cover design by www.spiffingcovers.com
Printed in the United Kingdom

Contents

Acknowledgements

I would like to thank my wife, Jenny, and my children, Josh, Zoe and Natasha for all the love and fun.

1
A Personal Story

I have often thought that people who buy books should be told exactly why a particular author has been approached to write about a given subject. So, at the outset I am going to write honestly about my particular experience of life and journey into faith, hoping that this will help you to understand where I'm coming from. Of course, Christian writers can only express their understanding of the faith through the filter of their personality and life circumstances – so please bear in mind that I regard myself (and am definitely regarded by others) as a bit extreme in certain respects! I am not claiming that my views are especially original or radical, but I alert you to this matter because the merits of what are more obviously my opinions (perhaps especially about the current state of the Church) need to be tested.

Like most evangelists, I am acquainted with the power of rhetorical flourish (some would say exaggeration). I could express myself in a more "balanced" way sometimes if I wanted to, but I don't. Jesus often used graphic language or imagery to warn and encourage us in the gospels. At least I find it easy to follow Him in this. I deliberately set some of what I have to say in sharp relief, so that what I take to be the main issues will stand out. I must also acknowledge that my understanding of so many things in this book has changed radically over time and I hope that my perception will continue to deepen as God leads me on. In short, I am trying to express what I really believe at this moment without fear, but want what I have written to be tested by you. My aim is that you will feel liberated to continue to pursue what many experience as *the great adventure* – our commission to preach the Gospel. If anything I write gets in the way, then I am sure you will feel free to disregard it.

A friend who read the manuscript of this book, and who evinces a much greater pastoral concern than I do, pointed out that there isn't much patient explaining of good ways to evangelise and that the examples of evangelism I do chose come from a very narrow context. I fear that both of these criticisms are fully justified, but I've decided not to do anything about it. There are many excellent books covering issues relating to techniques for effective evangelistic preaching and personal evangelism. If you want more detailed explanation you will certainly be able to find it. And I wanted to write a highly personalised and passionate book and not a text book about something I love, in the hope that God will speak through my particular experience. So there!

My journey to faith

Here's some personal background. My father's career was in local government and he applied for jobs that took us all over the country. However, wherever they lived, my parents always attended the local Anglican church. I remain very grateful to them for providing a loving and stable home, which nurtured and sustained me as I grew up. I knew without doubt that my parents loved me and there is, of course, no greater gift you can give a child. Although we went to church on Sundays, I can't say that I heard much about God in everyday life. He didn't seem to be relevant to the rest of the week.

My parents set a moral example, which was typically English and conservative middle-class – and therefore quasi-Christian in character. As I was growing up, this was reducible to "Be an honest boy, work hard and don't get anyone pregnant." But I would say that my parents, for all their years of church attendance, had little personal understanding or experience of Jesus. When my friends and I experimented with the Ouija board on the dining room table at home, my mother happily joined in. So, I would describe their faith as fairly nominal.

In many ways this was hardly surprising, given their experience of church. The vicar of one church which they attended for some 10 years had very little faith himself. When I was on the verge of leaving this church I tried to discuss my doubts with him, but he was strangely unwilling to comment. Much later, after I became a Christian, he told me that he didn't believe in the resurrection. As a family we were never able to focus on anything he said when he preached. He used to annoy my father and I by reading bits out of the newspaper, thus reminding us of what we could have been doing at home. I was also offended by the fact that he could never remember my name. Actually one day he did, but he attached it to my brother, which was bit of a blow.

I suppose the spiritual rot began to set in when I was about eleven years old. I knew that this vicar had experienced three breakdowns and, quite frankly, there seemed to be something wrong with him most of the time. But even more importantly, *the music in his church was terrible!* From the age of about eleven I developed a serious passion for pop music – and have subsequently failed to develop any appreciation for church, or any other kind of classical music. I know this makes me a total Philistine, and I am only openly acknowledging bestial ignorance, not wishing to score points against any other form of music. I have tried to change and every so often, when I make this kind of confession, a well-intentioned soul will give me a CD. But (don't tell anyone), I never put it on.

I really didn't (and don't) like organ music in particular and, of course, there was (and is) rather a lot of that in church. There was also the distinctively Anglican struggle with various hymn and coloured service books which used to leave me feeling physically challenged. And they would insist on delivering the whole service in a foreign language – 17th century English. Church seemed to me to be powerless, dull and incomprehensible. No wonder it made no impact on what we did for the rest of the week as a family! When I reached the age of consent (around 12 years old according to my mother), I gladly stopped going. Although I am an ordained member of the Church of England, my attitude to the national Church is still shaped by these initial experiences.

The next significant stage in my spiritual development came as I worked for a religious studies O-level. Having grown up in church and presumably Sunday school (though I have no memories whatsoever of the latter), I knew quite a lot of the text of the New Testament and therefore thought I would have no trouble doing well in this subject. I did the course with about 7 other boys at my grammar school, some of whom were Christians (I think), but none of whom had credibility in the cruel school world in which our sense of self-worth so often takes a beating.

It soon became obvious that the writer of the course material we had to study didn't believe in the so-called miraculous events described in the gospels and neither did our teacher. Apparently, we could accept that Jesus fed 5,000 from a few bits of bread and fish if we wished (subtext: if we were intellectually feeble). Or we could accept that it was inherently unlikely that Jews would have travelled without food for the day (subtext: if we had half a brain cell). Given this objection to the more obvious meaning of the text, we should look for "the deeper significance" of the story – which was clearly that *sharing is important*. Jesus was such an incredible person that He could persuade everyone to share their food and we should share too. Well, of course, that was easier to believe – just as it was easier to believe that Jesus was really walking on a sand bar and not actually on water. Naturally, the disciples had made a mistake in the dim moonlight. Presumably, the "deeper significance" is that we too should be the kind of people who walk on the sand bars of life – though only in the moonlight of course!

So the dinosaur that is post-enlightenment rationalism roamed wild and free around our school. Surely we couldn't believe in miracles in an age of electric light bulbs! I followed the logic through and quickly came to realise that if there were no miraculous events, there was no resurrection, and if there was no resurrection then Jesus was nothing more than a sad martyr of 2,000 years ago. If this was the case then, clearly, He had no particular relevance to my life. I became an agnostic and then graduated to atheism with a little help from my friends. I studied and practised the occult (to a small degree) and studied various other religions and philosophies. I became convinced that there was no overarching purpose to life and, if anything, I agreed with Freud that people's behaviour is largely governed consciously or otherwise by their sexual drives. Of course, the fact that I resonated with this said more about me than other people.

Teenage life became increasingly dominated by the pursuit of girls, success at school and at sport (tennis in the summer, football in the winter) and music. I became increasingly good at all of it and reflected a lot on "the meaning" of my own abilities. Some teenagers can be really pretentious can't they? I remember asking my mother why, compared with other people, everything I touched seemed to turn to gold. When I was seventeen I tore ligaments in my knee, but apart from this, it is difficult to remember any really bad thing that happened when I was growing up.

I felt no need for belief in a god. I was, however, aware that when I achieved something (like getting into Oxford University or putting a band together) I remained unsatisfied. I thought that if I could just reach the next peak then I would be content. But having reached it, I never was. I accepted one Christian tenet, which is that humans try to put themselves at the centre of the universe. I knew I did and I believed that others did too, no matter how nice they appeared to be on the outside. This lack of peace, despite achievement, and the awareness of my own selfishness were to become important when I first met Christians and heard the Gospel.

When I went to university to study law, I soon realised that having been a big fish in a small pond, I was now a tiny tiddler in a massive ocean. The self-possession, savoir-faire and invulnerability of the public school students around me left me feeling very insecure. Nothing I had previously put my confidence in really counted for anything in this context, because many of my contemporaries could do any or all of it better than I could. Naturally, I thought about going home and even told my parents I was quitting. I sat on the stairs leading up my tutor's room, turning the question over in my mind just once more before going to inform him. I saw a spider climbing up a thread hanging down from his web and then followed the fine example of Robert the Bruce in matters of guidance. I decided that since the spider had the courage to struggle on, so would I!

The only people who stood out to me as being different from the rest were the Christians I met at university. They seemed to have a different source of confidence. I engaged with them through intellectual debate about the existence of God, but I was drawn to them as people. They made an impact by their response to me as a person and not by the answers they gave in the debate. Some didn't understand the faith sufficiently well to answer my questions and I guess that I wasn't initially in a place where I could hear what they were saying in any case.

There was one Christian girl at college that my non-Christian friends and I used to refer to as "the girl with the shining face" for obvious reasons. There was another girl we called "the poison dwarf". I think that speaks for itself as well. Everyone else in college sought to avoid "the poison dwarf" apart from "the girl with the shining face". Initially I thought, "Well, it's because *you're a Christian*." in other words, "Because you're a bit naïve." But I had one conversation with the girl with the shining face in which it became obvious that she knew exactly how poisonous the other girl could be, but she still chose to spend time with her. That really made an impact on me.

A long process ensued in which I began to re-examine Christianity, especially after I met a lawyer who said there was quite a lot of evidence in history that Jesus had been raised from the dead. He recommended a book entitled *Who Moved the Stone?* by a lawyer called Frank Morrison, which discusses the evidence. However, the author appeared to me to presuppose that the biblical accounts were true and I couldn't accept that. Slowly, though, I became more convinced and joined the Christian Union, which at that time in Keble College was pretty large and effective. I remember sitting and listening during the Bible studies having absolutely nothing to say, but wanting to drink the whole thing in. I went to a concert given by a couple of Christians. I hated the music, but during a brief conversation with the singer afterwards, the look of compassion in her eyes was too much for me and I left. I continued to take one step forward and two steps back.

I was invited to attend an Easter programme for teenagers based at a school called Northforeland. I was even asked to give a testimony and went through it in written form with a friend just beforehand.

He informed me that it was "a bit boring". Someone spoke before I did and she did really well and then it was my turn. I disregarded my boring written testimony and spoke off the top of my head. I have no recollection of what I said, but remember the feeling of power going out of me and then coming round at the end! It was as if I had been watching myself speak. Amazingly, some became Christians that night – but I'm not sure that I was one.

The clinching moment came during Mission England, when one of Billy Graham's talks was relayed by video link to Oxford town hall. I went with a friend who was already preparing to go into the Anglican ministry. The more Billy spoke, the more it seemed to me that Jesus was in the room. I lost all awareness of anything else and recognised a presence that had come to me years before. Over the Christmas period one year there had been a family argument and I went for a walk in the countryside to try and calm down. I became aware of a presence offering me an invitation to be with Him. It was an offer made with complete vulnerability and I declined and walked on. I now recognised the same presence in and around Billy Graham as he spoke in his very simple way about Jesus. I understood something from his talk that I had never taken on board before, which was that I needed to make Jesus Lord of my life if I was to become a Christian. Billy invited people to come to the front if they had prayed the prayer of commitment. I felt like the building had been shaken and was also aware of an enormous power pulling me out of my seat. But I held onto it and refused to go.

On the way home, my friend and I had a disagreement about something and he suggested that we pray together before we parted. I had never prayed with anyone before, but couldn't really get out of it. We sat in a couple of chairs in my room and he prayed a surprising prayer: "Thank you, Lord, that John can speak in tongues." My friend was a conservative evangelical who did not speak in tongues himself, but who obviously felt moved to pray in this way on this occasion. He was as surprised as I was when I began to do so. As I did, I had the most ecstatic experience of my life and it lasted about 40 seconds. I felt completely filled with love and in that moment my life was changed.

In fact, I was probably converted before that night, but it was only afterwards that spiritual things came to life in my experience. I discovered an immediate need to read the Bible and that when I prayed, it was as if I was actually getting through to someone. I also cried my way through church services at St Aldate's in Oxford. I didn't feel happy or sad, but couldn't stop crying! This went on for several weeks and I interpret it as relief on the part of my spirit/soul that I had finally been brought back home.

I was filled with an immense passion to speak about the faith that I now definitely had and, of course, this is where my experience of evangelism began. In fact, God seemed to show me almost immediately that He was calling me to preach the Gospel and I spent most of my time doing so when I wasn't studying law. I also continued to attend those teenage house parties at Northforeland and was taught by a couple of Pentecostals more about the Holy Spirit. Within a very short time, I had seen the sick healed and demons cast out and many others filled with the Spirit with my own eyes. These things happened as we invited the Spirit to come and touch the young people we were responsible for. I immediately wanted to do this stuff at university! But this caused quite a lot of consternation amongst my more conservative friends at college who had been taught to be hesitant about the gifts of the Spirit. But we held together because of a common desire to see people converted to Jesus Christ.

I made some terrible mistakes during these first few years, but I committed myself to being teachable and set out to learn how to become as effective as possible in preaching the Gospel. After I completed my law degree, I went on to work as a lay assistant in three different churches and it was during this time that I heard Michael Green and J. John preach evangelistically. This book is dedicated to them because they are the most gifted evangelists I have ever heard and because they inspired me to evangelise. In truth, I have never thought to emulate Michael's style – not least because it comes with such erudition and an incredible use of the Bible. I found John's style slightly more accessible as a model, because he is a little ruder and uses humour so powerfully. My best talks and illustrations to date have all been based on theirs!

I trained at Wycliffe theological college to become a vicar, but didn't go on to be ordained because of a broken engagement. I went from college to assist Nicky and Sila Lee (who were then leading a church plant from Holy Trinity Brompton) in an unordained capacity. I finally became ordained and am currently leading a church with my wife in central London.

Throughout this time, my twin passions have continued to be preaching the Gospel and encouraging people to be open to the power of the Spirit. I have expressed these passions in this country and abroad – to individuals and to large meetings. I believe in the intellectual credibility of the central Christian truth claims – that Jesus is the Son of God as demonstrated by His resurrection from the dead. I believe that an ongoing and powerful experience of the Holy Spirit is fundamental to the Christian life and to every ministry. There is so much more I could say, but I hope this gives you enough useful information against which to test what I have to write. I don't mind if you disagree; you go your way and I'll go God's (only joking!).

A final thought: in the course of this book you will read of various ways in which God has used me over the years. These wonderful stories serve to illustrate only one thing, which is that if God can use *me* in these kinds of ways he can surely use you. I am not proud of what I am going to tell you, but I do want you to know that I have continued to fail in various ways since I've become a Christian. I had a longstanding addiction to sex prior to conversion (including the use of pornography) which I continued to struggle with for some time after I became a Christian. My wife and I had a courtship that made Romeo and Juliet seem like a light romantic comedy – full of agony and ecstasy. I found that in my excitement at being with her, vomiting tended to ensue. I told you I was a bit extreme! Anyway, at one stage, I stupidly got engaged to someone else and when I broke off that engagement there was a great deal of pain. I have also been involved in major relational breakdown with a particular group of Christians. There was a deep disagreement about a particular course of action and, as I write, this isn't really resolved. I could go on about my weaknesses and failures, but I hope you get the idea. I also know what it is to suffer in various ways. My mother died when I was twenty-two, shortly after I became a Christian, and when she died I lost my closest friend. But God showed Himself to be faithful to me in this situation and although it was very painful, this was undoubtedly a formative experience in my life of faith.

God has used me to bring many people to him and he has used me to bring the power of the Spirit to individuals and churches with little or no experience of His power. I have also let God down, let those I love down, and failed to live up to the very Gospel I proclaim. In saying this, I do not mean to condone my sinfulness, or yours, but I do mean to speak of the kindness and the grace of God who appears to take a long-term view about our growth into the image of Christ. My experience and my study of the Bible reveal that God can use anyone who seeks Him to advance His Kingdom – even people like you and me. My prayer is that this book will encourage us to continue to do so.

2
Evangelism as a Priority

From an evangelist's perspective, it's a very good time to be alive! This land needs evangelists as never before. Surely it's better to have a gift that's actually needed than to have to hang around waiting for your time to come? Church history teaches us that "the darkest time is just before dawn" and since our current situation is so dire, surely the light must be about to shine? Perhaps we shall see the light of the Gospel shine out in a new way in the next few years. What a privilege.

It could easily be argued that the West is in the process of growing out of Christianity. A trend towards decline has been gathering pace from the 1960s onwards. The survey evidence suggests that even those church movements that are still growing are adding fewer people than they once did. Many church movements are in radical decline.

But is it Christianity that Britain is moving away from? I'm not sure that our country has *really* considered and rejected anything other than a twisted caricature of Christianity. But British people certainly don't like what they have experienced of the Church. In fact, I think it would be fair to say that the country as whole has taken a good look at the Church and found it wanting. If I want to establish common ground with the people I regularly preach to, I need only describe my negative experiences of church as a child.

75% of people under the age of 25 have never been to church – which reflects the feelings of their parents. Teenagers in our country don't ignore church because they are anti-authoritarian and rebellious. They aren't interested because their parents aren't interested; and they aren't interested because when they went it wasn't interesting! Perhaps there has been confusion in the British mind between the Church and the Gospel, between religion and faith, *but who can blame the British for confusing these things?* After all, isn't the Church supposed to bear witness to the power and vitality of the Gospel? We don't seem to do that to any great extent.

I know this is a bit depressing! I do not mean to denigrate the incredible impact of some churches and also of some evangelists over the last 30 years. It's not my place (or anyone else's) to write off the work of God through His people. But the inescapable conclusion is that we haven't done church very well in this country for quite a long time now and people have clearly voted with their feet. If we were a business, there would be a radical review as a result of which many outlets would be shut down. I have worked in four large churches and although there has definitely been growth through conversion in them all, they mainly grew, or are growing, by adding Christian, or at least "Christianised", people.

This general picture may be influenced by profound social factors, like the impact of the wars on two generations, either decimating it numerically or destroying it spiritually (how could God allow so much suffering to come to us?). It is arguable that we have never reached whole strata of the population in a significant way – for instance, the urbanised poor or those left outside the rapidly developing towns during the social upheavals of the Industrial Revolution.

And there are other factors. Without wishing to be rude to anyone (but being at least direct), the mainline churches seem to have been beset by weak and vacillating leadership. Maybe the unseen but extremely powerful structures around high profile leaders stop them making the impact they would like to make. George Carey warned at the beginning of his time as Archbishop that there was a possibility that people would see the Church of England as a toothless old woman talking to herself in the corner to whom no one is listening. Without blaming any specific individuals, is it not true that we have, as a Church, passed from serious possibility into grim reality? This seems to apply to all the main denominations.

The process of theological training has probably damaged quite a few bright eyed leaders in the more established traditions. The liberal academic agenda with its insistence on radical scepticism often proves difficult to resist – even though it is intellectually suspect. A woefully inadequate model of what it means to do church or mission certainly doesn't help those preparing to lead. Poorly equipped leaders tend to pass on ineffective models to their people. The older denominations are often hampered by out-dated rules relating to worship, church government and organisation. We are generally stuck trying to make something work that may have been more appropriate to an earlier era of our history, but which most people now find alienating.

I regard myself as a charismatic first, second, third, fourth and fifth. But in churches where we like to think of ourselves as being "led by the Spirit" there is often an isolationist culture. That is to say, we have ways of behaving and speaking that are unnecessarily removed from the ways of those people who live around us. How many leaders could introduce a song, service, or time of prayer without descending into spiritual clichés? How many people in church could explain the basics of their faith without experiencing similar problems of expression and therefore of communication? If we can't resolve these kinds of issues then we shouldn't expect to see people coming to our churches in any large number. Why would "outsiders" want to join us if they can't understand what's going on? When we can't even explain to them what we believe in a common language? This is the focus of Paul's concern in his first letter to the Corinthians, in which he emphasises the value of prophecy over tongues in the worship context, precisely because tongues is comprehensible to outsiders (1 Corinthians 14:22-25).

We so often have very strong concerns about issues that are of limited importance. I believe that churches should have a short little span of attention when it comes to distinctive beliefs, for instance. We should focus on Jesus crucified and risen and on the gift of the Spirit freely given to all who believe. These are our essential truth claims. There are no other issues for which our churches should be known – not our baptismal policy, attitude to spiritual warfare, view of the place of Israel, view of the role of women, doctrines of hell or the Second Coming. Obviously, we shall all have our opinions about these and many other things, but we need to keep them in check because they are of secondary importance.

I know that many individuals and churches want evangelism to be a priority and seek to make it so. But are we really prepared for what it takes to be open to non-Christians? We desperately need to re-imagine the way we live and the way we do church for the sake of an alienated culture. But that would involve radical change. Are we ready for the change that would be needed to the way we do things if serious pagan hordes actually turned up? I hate to say this, but I doubt it.

If the Church was going to write a book the title would be, "We have never done things that way before". I know of one man who was sacked from three different churches because he succeeded in bringing large numbers of teenagers into the life of the churches he worked for. The leaders and congregations of these churches were not prepared for the changes made inevitable by the presence of "real outsiders".

Of course, evangelism has to be a priority for us at all times and in all places. We have to be ready to preach the Gospel in and out of season (2 Timothy 4:2). In other words, when things are going well and when they aren't. If we are to be imitators of Christ or Christians (literally "little Christs") then we shall surely attempt to do what He did. Now, it isn't terribly difficult to spot what Jesus spent most of His time doing. All the active years of His ministry were taken up announcing the message of the Kingdom to the people of God (Matthew 4:23). When He wasn't doing that He appears to have been sleeping, praying or talking to His disciples.

Jesus committed this message of the Kingdom to His closest disciples within the time span of His earthly ministry (Matthew 10:35-10:1; 5-7). He then commanded His first followers to, *"Go and make disciples of all nations, baptising them in the name of the Father, and of the Son and of the Holy Spirit and teaching them to obey everything I have commanded you"* (Matthew 28:19-20). Fortunately, He doesn't intend to just leave us to get on with the task. It is the promise of Jesus that He will work with us in the harvest fields of the world:

"Surely I am with you always, to the very end of the age." (Matthew 28:20b).

Indeed, it is His mission that we are engaged in.

I do not believe that there is a more central statement of our purpose than what is often called the "Great Commission" at the end of Matthew's gospel. Neither is there a more vital promise. We are called to this particular task, but we can only seek to fulfil it in the power of the Spirit. We know that just making converts is not enough. Who is interested merely in a show of hands, or in people coming to the front at the end of an evangelistic event? The real deal is to find ways of making disciples – those who are committed to following in the way of the Master. But all disciples begin as converts and this is where evangelists come in.

Churches should always seek to release their evangelists to make their distinctive contribution to the work of the church, and the need to do this in Britain has probably never been greater. Church leaders ought to seek to release and encourage the evangelists entrusted to them. And evangelists ought to bring to the leaders of their churches what they feel called to do. We need the wisdom that is usually to be gained from those who are over us in the Lord. *But ultimately evangelists usually do not and should not be expected to wait forever for churches to release them.* Sadly, evangelists often find themselves doing what their hand finds to do and then praying that the fruit of their work will be incorporated into the church at some stage. Indeed, evangelists often go through this process of starting something, being ignored and then incorporated later – even when God is clearly blessing what they are doing! We must be willing to take risks and to encourage others who are doing so – especially at the moment, as we struggle to find effective means of evangelising in a bewildering culture.

It seems to me more noble to see the need and fail somewhat in seeking to meet it, than to see the need and do nothing, or seek to meet the need in such a way that the need actually increases! Most of those who have been truly used by God have begun as failures and all of them have tasted failure. A good evangelist is a bad evangelist who got better. I believe that we are in a place of collective evangelistic failure. Now is the time for us all to get a lot better.

3
What is the Gospel?

If we are going to proclaim the Gospel of Jesus, we must first understand what it is. Paul wails in deep distress, *"Even if an angel from heaven should preach a gospel other than the one we preached to you, let him be eternally condemned!"* (Galatians 1:8). He is afraid that the impact of false teaching in the Church is causing the Galatians to lose connection with the Gospel of Jesus. Clearly, we need to be sure that it is in fact the authentic Gospel that we are preaching.

Actually, I was once accused of "preaching another gospel" in this sense because I insisted on seeking to hold together the proclamation of the Gospel with a demonstration of the power of the Spirit. Surely this is highly ironic, given Paul's insistence in this very letter that experience of the Spirit is a validation of the Gospel he proclaimed: *"Does God give you his Spirit and work miracles amongst you because you observe the law or because you believe what you heard?"* (Galatians 3:5). However, like me, you have probably come across representations of the Christian message which seem at best only tangentially connected to the Gospel as it has been traditionally understood. So, in this chapter I want us to consider the fundamental question, what is the Gospel?

The Good News of Jesus

It is well known that our word "gospel" translates the Greek phrase *to euaggelion* and means "the good news". So what context does the New Testament give to the good news?

I will attempt to demonstrate from a consideration of the contexts in which the term "gospel" occurs in the New Testament that the good news is fundamentally *good news about the person of Jesus*. The gospels reveal that the Messiah is here right now! The well-attested fact that He died and rose again and that Jesus continues to be near to all who call upon Him is the essence of the news in Acts and ever thereafter. There is a movement from Jesus as the announcer of news about Himself to the Apostles as the announcers of the news about Him. However, because the Gospel and Jesus are so closely connected, He continues to be immediately at work when it is preached.

I think that we need to begin by reminding ourselves what it was about Jesus that made the authors of the New Testament think He was such good news. This requires an appreciation of Jesus in His particular context.

It is well known that at the time of Jesus, the people of Israel were groaning under the weight of Gentile occupation. Unlike so many surrounding nations who almost welcomed this foreign government because of the benefits that came with Roman rule, tiny Israel continually stirred up rebellion against the world super power. In the year of Jesus' birth, yet another band of His compatriots was crucified in Galilee for insurrection.

First century Israel was fiercely monotheistic and when symbols of emperor worship were erected in the temple at Jerusalem, the governor responsible was hastily called back to Rome and forbidden to do such a thing again. The Roman occupiers, who tended towards religious tolerance, couldn't but interpret this exclusivity of belief as atheism in practice because of the inherent rejection of the Roman pantheon. The Jews of Jesus' day longed for deliverance from unclean Gentile domination and for God to establish His Kingdom amongst them. Many were tormented by the question of how could God continue to allow His land to be polluted by Gentile filth!

We could say that there were several alternative theories as to *how* the Kingdom was to come, but that *it had to come* was not in dispute amongst many of the religious groupings of the day. The Pharisees attempted to take the holiness values of the Law from the confines of the temple and out to the people. The Essenes set themselves apart from what they saw as a corrupt nation by withdrawing into the desert to await the Teacher of Righteousness who would come and establish the Kingdom. The Zealots attempted to hasten the coming of the Kingdom by violent action. Lots of people had an interest in the coming of the Kingdom at the time of Jesus! The essential preparatory message of John the Baptist is about the coming of the Kingdom (Matthew 3:1-2).

So, first and foremost, Jesus is good news within this national and religious context. In fact, the writers of the New Testament make it clear that He is the Messianic Servant in whom is fulfilled all the national and religious aspirations of Israel, the historic people of God. Good news indeed for those hoping for the saving activity of God in their midst. Luke makes this connection between Jesus and the whole history of God's relationship explicit at the commencement of His ministry in Luke 4:14f.

In the careers of the great and the good, there comes a defining moment at which, looking back, we can see that the heart of their message has been revealed. Think of the great speeches of history given by leaders like Winston Churchill or Martin Luther-King, delivered at crucial times. Luke describes for us a defining moment of this kind in the ministry of Jesus. We might capture something of the distinctive local impact of what Jesus said in the synagogue on that day if we were to try to imagine that we too had grown up in Nazareth and that we were there.

Nazareth was a nothing village in a nowhere place. If you had grown up there you would have known all the nobodies who lived there (including Jesus) and you would have attended the synagogue every Saturday. At this time, all the talk would have been about the local boy made good, who had far surpassed anyone's expectations. After all, He was only the carpenter's son. But now He has become a *cause célèbre*; most in the region have heard of Him and everyone has an opinion (Luke 4:14-15). You have already heard Him speak and His teaching is extraordinary. It seems to resonate with all that you have grown up believing, but there is something different as well. Perhaps the wisdom of the ages dressed in the clothes of revolution. His beautiful words have already exposed and disturbed you, healed and shocked you, all at the same time. No one knows where He got such a depth of wisdom. Naturally, when He returns home, He is invited to speak in the local synagogue (Luke 4:16).

What will the young rabbi say? He is offered the scroll of the prophet Isaiah and reads from the ancient text:

"The Spirit of the Lord is on me because he has anointed me to preach good news to the poor. He has sent me to proclaim freedom for the prisoners and recovery of sight to the blind, to release the oppressed and to proclaim the year of the Lord's favour." (Luke 4:18-19)

These words would have been very familiar to you; indeed you may well have memorised them as a child. They evoke the ache of hope – hope of a coming Servant of the Lord who will set His own people free. The wider context of this passage from Isaiah is about a return from exile for the people of God in which the messenger, anointed by God's Spirit, announces the kingly rule of God. Isaiah prophesies nothing less than the dawning of a new age in which the day of salvation will finally arrive. There will be untrammelled joy (Isaiah 61:3), a restoration of all that has been broken down in the land (61:4), and the people of God will be recompensed for all that has gone before (Isaiah 61:7).

Jesus finishes reading from the ancient text and everyone in the synagogue is electrified. What new meaning will the rabbi bring or what new application? Not merely a new meaning or a new application, but a new and defining moment: *"Today, this scripture has been fulfilled in your hearing"* (Luke 4:21). That can only mean one thing: He claims to be the Servant of the Lord, the one that Isaiah foresaw hundreds of years before. This is the tremendous good news of the actual presence of the Messiah.

The Servant would be specially anointed by the Spirit (Luke 4:18). The kings of Israel had always been anointed with oil to show that the Spirit of the Lord was upon them. Luke tells us that the Spirit descended on Jesus at His baptism (Luke 3:21). He performed extraordinary acts of power from that day onwards. In the very next synagogue, Jesus casts out a demon right in the middle of the service (Luke 4:31-37)! The Servant has been anointed with spiritual power for specific purposes such as these. He has been sent to "release the oppressed" (Luke 4:18). The Messianic Servant makes a personal impact on the people of God. Jesus comes to deal with emotional and spiritual poverty, personal imprisonment and blindness as He announces the good news of His own presence or coming.

Not only does He proclaim the good news of His coming "to the poor" (Luke 4:18) but He also demonstrates the goodness of the news in personal terms. Jesus does not merely speak of God's forgiveness – He forgives real people. He does not merely declare freedom – He breaks down the walls of imprisonment and sets particular captives free. He doesn't merely speak of healing – He heals actual blind people. The good news is of the presence or coming of a person and is experienced personally. *"If I drive out demons by the finger of God, then the Kingdom of God has come upon you"* (Luke 11:20).

I believe that Jesus *increasingly came to understand* that He was the Messiah. Of course, I am not suggesting that Jesus was "adopted" as the Son of God at His baptism, but that as a child and then a young person He could not have known everything there was to know about His identity and purpose. No real child or young person does. Was it the experience of the Spirit and the voice from heaven at His baptism that finally convinced Him? Is that why He was driven off into the desert straight afterwards, to come to terms with what He now knew for certain?

I believe that the Spirit revealed to the Son what the Messiah must do through His own deep study of the Old Testament Scriptures. We see a deliberate prophetic enactment of the Messianic role throughout the gospels. Consider the cleansing of the temple, the healing of the sick, the fulfilment of the law motif in His teaching or the triumphal entry. Consider the choosing of twelve disciples to replace the twelve tribes of Israel, His personal claim to be the true Temple, the vine and the true Israel. As the Messiah, Jesus realises that everything in Israel's history has pointed to Him and will culminate in Him, including the sacrificial system. He is the Suffering Servant of Isaiah who will be despised and rejected, who will be pierced for our transgressions, but whose bones will not be broken and who will see the vindication of a new day.

So the good news is first and foremost of the presence or coming of Jesus as Messiah to the historic people of God in order to set them free. We shall return to the theme of the proclamation of the Gospel and cultural relevance in chapter six, but I feel we need to understand this particular context if we are going to be effective in our own communication of the Gospel.

Clearly, there is much fruitful source material here for dialogue with religious Jews who know and love the Old Testament. Arguments from the Old Testament dominate the initial presentations of the Gospel in Acts – but what about those who are unfamiliar with the Old Testament and with Jewish history? We need to appreciate how distinctively Jewish is the setting of Jesus' ministry if we are to take up effectively the challenge of proclaiming the Gospel of Jesus in a non-Jewish context today.

The Gospel in Mark And Paul

Mark's Gospel is generally taken to be the earliest and he uses the phrase "the good news" more than anyone else. Of course, in a general sense, everything recorded in the gospels is part of the Gospel and that certainly includes an account of Jesus' teaching, miracles, and (in Mark particularly) the death of Jesus. What emerges from the New Testament texts is that there is a consistency about the facts of the story of Jesus in the proclamation of the Apostles. The degree to which the focus is on Jesus as Messiah or Jesus as universal Saviour depends on the context – Jewish or Gentile. The contrast is very clear between the evangelistic sermons of Peter and Paul in Acts 2 and 17. The presentation of the story of Jesus must be made appropriate to Jerusalem and to Athens.

But the centrality of Jesus Himself to the good news is maintained throughout Mark's gospel. Indeed, to lose one's life for the sake of Jesus is to lose one's life for the Gospel (Mark 8:35). To leave behind home and family for Jesus' sake is to leave them behind for the sake of the Gospel (Mark 10:49). Mark is setting out to write the "Gospel of Jesus" (1:1); Jesus and the Gospel are one. Paul tends to call the Gospel "God's good news" and also suggests that the facts of the Gospel story have a fixed content in that the Gospel can be announced, talked over, made known or put forward for discussion. But he also calls it the good news of Christ:

> *"Now when I went to Troas to preach the Gospel of Christ and found that the Lord had opened a door for me."* (2 Corinthians 2:12)

Also in 2 Corinthians 9:13:

> *"Because of the service by which you have proved yourselves, men will praise God for the obedience that accompanies our confession of the Gospel of Christ."*

So the Gospel is a declaration of the facts about Jesus – who He is and what He has done for us. But also the Gospel is Jesus – His present power to make effective in our lives what He made real in Galilee or Capernaum.

"Witness" Language in Acts

Before the Ascension, the disciples are commissioned (Luke 24:45f) and they are commanded to "bear witness" to "these things" about Jesus – the death and resurrection of the Christ and the need for repentance and faith. Of course, they will have to be empowered to be witnesses and this will happen when the Holy Spirit comes upon them (Acts 1:8). Luke tends to use the word "witness" to describe those who were with Jesus when He was alive, though He extends this category to include Stephen and Paul on the basis of their visionary experiences of the risen Christ (Acts 22:20; 22:15). Witnesses clearly need to attest accurately "the facts" of the Jesus story. They were there to see the miracles, hear the teaching, mourn the death and hail the resurrection. Indeed they are compelled to bear witness to their experiences because they know that what they are talking about really happened. John says to the Sanhedrin,

> "Judge for yourselves whether it is right in God's sight to obey you rather than God. For we cannot help speaking about what we have seen and heard." (Acts 4:19)

However, because the Gospel and Jesus are so closely connected, there must also be the closest possible connection between Jesus and His witnesses. This means that for Luke, personal encounter with Jesus is indispensable to the proclamation of the Gospel, because the Gospel is all about the person of Jesus.

Conclusions About the Gospel

I deduce from all this that the good news is of the person of Jesus. Primarily, in the gospels, this is the good news of the coming of the Messianic Servant to the historic people of Israel. In Mark and Paul (who are the main users of the phrase *to euaggelion*) the good news continues to be the good news of Jesus. In Acts, witnesses of the Gospel have had a personal encounter with Jesus. So Jesus Himself is the primary content of the news. However, the good news is also the more objective account of what Jesus did in history on our behalf and the presentation of the story will vary considerably according to context – Jewish or Gentile.

What then can we say about the proclamation of the Gospel on the basis of these conclusions?

1) We Need to Keep Jesus at the Centre of the Proclamation

Paul says to the Corinthians,

> "When I came to you, brothers, I did not come with eloquence or

superior wisdom as I proclaimed to you the testimony about God. For I resolved to know nothing while I was with you except Jesus Christ and him crucified." (1 Corinthians 2:1-2)

Jesus is the centre of the proclamation, both who He is and what He has done for us. We know that Christian claims about the uniqueness of Jesus' identity and the significance of His death on the cross are difficult for many to hear. They get at the heart of our arrogance and self-focus. Like Paul, we sometimes need to "resolve" to keep these things at the centre. By the way, the apostle isn't rejecting rhetorical technique or powerful oratory in these verses, he's rejecting the emptiness of these things in themselves. In other words, there is no power (as the Greeks seemed to think) in fine sounding words! However, "Jesus Christ and Him crucified" is the power of the Gospel and therefore Paul says that he deliberately made these the focus of his preaching when he went to Corinth. I'm sure he preached with great oratorical and rhetorical impact when he was there though!

But we must resist every attempt to make anything other than Jesus the focus of the Gospel. For instance, the idea that people ought to love one another is not the Gospel. Firstly, although Jesus does teach us to love our neighbour as ourselves (Matthew 22:39), we don't actually need Him to tell us this. In fact, most of the religions of the world agree that we ought to try and love one another. Many atheists and agnostics agree that we ought to love one another. Of course, we all discover that it is easier said than done, this loving business, hence our need of the releasing power of Jesus' death on the cross. But most communities seek to found themselves upon a corporate love ethic. When we say that people ought to love one another, we aren't proclaiming the Gospel.

I once went to a church were the "Evangelism Committee" spent it's time deciding how much money to give to various projects aimed at helping the poor. It is obviously important that churches give money to the poor, but when we do so we aren't actually evangelising anyone. Evangelism has to do with the proclamation of Jesus and Him crucified. No proclamation, no evangelism.

I am not convinced that the "spiritual warfare" which we are called to as Christians has much to do with prayer. Though prayer which is focused on Jesus, His glory and His power to save, is essential to every effective evangelistic enterprise, we enter into direct conflict with the enemy by preaching the Gospel, healing the sick and casting out demons. No proclamation, no evangelism.

This is probably the pedantic old lawyer in me, but I think that "servant evangelism", in which we do surprisingly nice things for people like washing their cars when they haven't asked us to, is surely misnamed. Acts of service of this kind may lead to opportunities for explanation (though I suspect that the cynical English would often see through what is going on), but I still say, *no proclamation, no evangelism!* We must beware of every subtle and totally unconscious attempt to help us evade the challenge of preaching Christ and Him crucified. People liked Jesus when He healed and fed them; they were less keen when He made direct statements about His identity, purpose, and the implications for the way that life should be lived.

In the same way, it is difficult for me to see any sense in which the mere performance of liturgical services in church could possibly be described as preaching the Gospel. A bishop once explained to a colleague of mine why he was going to keep a church going as it was, even though no one attended the services except the priest! The answer was that the daily performance of the mass fulfilled the mission of the church. This causes me to wonder whether the Bishop had ever read the New Testament. There is obviously some emphasis in the New Testament on Jesus' final meal with His disciples as the basis for a distinctive Christian act of corporate worship. But how could anyone look upon something so personal to the community of believers and see there the main vehicle of mission to the world? No proclamation of Jesus in terms that people outside the church can receive, no Gospel.

2) We Need to Translate the Story of Jesus into the Language of our Context

What relevance do words like "Messiah ... Kingdom of God ... Servant of the Lord ... sin ... repentance ... Son of Man" have for those outside Judaism? Does the proclamation of this language have power in itself, just because it is in the New Testament? The power of the Gospel does not exist in word formulae, but in the person of Jesus. I suggest that because we have relied on various word formulae, either from the Jewish New Testament context or from specific church liturgical contexts, the Gospel has been deprived of its power. The idea that we must do church services in a particular way because we always have (as though there is a necessary connection between spiritual power and age) simply reflects a failure to engage with our fundamental task. The Church has always been called to adapt the proclamation of the message so that it can be heard in the culture of the day. We face exactly the same challenge today – and so will those coming after us.

Of course, we need to communicate about Jesus using words, but we shall see that the words chosen by those who first preached the Gospel outside of Israel were fairly different from those used by Jesus Himself, or by those evangelising Jews (see chapter six). Jesus understood the universal dimensions of His ministry, but He saw Himself as having come historically to the people of Israel (Mark 7:27). He chooses His language accordingly. Unless we are called to ministry amongst the Jews, we need to go with the good news of

Jesus, not the obscure news of ancient Jewish religious formularies. Those who evangelised Gentiles in Acts never referred to the Old Testament in their proclamation of the Gospel. Why do we need the obscure religious formularies of 17th century England when no one speaks King James' English anymore?

We need to undertake the difficult task of proclaiming Jesus and the facts about His life, teaching, miracles, death and resurrection in a culturally relevant way. We cannot extricate a transcendental Jesus who is wholly removed from His history. But we have to present Jesus as being of universal relevance and as being of crucial important to the lives of people who know nothing of the New Testament context. We need categories of language which take us beyond the language of the New Testament if we are to speak authentically to people in our very different culture. We'll return to this when we think about evangelistic preaching in chapter eight.

3) We Need to Be Witnesses of Jesus

The power of the Gospel does not reside in the correct exposition of a particular theory of the atonement, but in the person of Jesus. That is why God has been able to use evangelists who have had fairly different understandings of the atonement (amongst many other things!) A young Christian once said to me that he couldn't understand how God was choosing to use a particular church because it taught the wrong doctrine of hell. Precise formulation of every area of theology is not as important as an appropriate presentation of Jesus. Anyway, I presume that this church didn't spend a lot of time proclaiming its aberrant doctrine of hell, to the great relief of the congregation, no doubt!

Witnesses do need to know the facts of the story of Jesus, as we have seen. But the concept of "witness" in Acts has a personal dimension too. Stephen and Paul are included amongst the witnesses because of their encounter with the risen Christ – one at his martyrdom and the other at his conversion. We need to bear witness to Jesus Himself. In other words, when we are evangelising I believe that Jesus makes a strong identification with us. After all, He is the message we proclaim.

I am not suggesting that we become one with Christ when we are evangelising, but I do believe that we are "in Christ" to use the phrase ubiquitously found in the Pauline material and that He is in us. Therefore, when we "hold out the Word of Life" (Philippians 2:16), we may sometimes be aware of the immediate presence of Jesus by His Spirit. Most of us who have preached the Gospel know of times when we seem to be observing ourselves or listening to ourselves as we speak. We can be particularly aware that we are being "carried along by the Spirit". We may become aware of a special concentration or attentiveness or impact of the Spirit on our hearers. We may know that the power of the Lord is there to save.

In the course of preaching the Gospel, I have been told on occasion that I sound like Jesus and that my hands are just like Jesus' hands! I have also sensed a feeling of awe or wonder when I've started to talk to some non-Christians afterwards. Of course, we all know that these are not responses to me and I don't take them personally. I believe that these are direct responses by people to the presence of Jesus in me on those occasions. I find it very interesting that intelligent people who could not claim to have the first idea what Jesus looked or sounded like, want to make this identification. I believe it is because they sense the presence of Jesus as His Gospel (and therefore He Himself) is being proclaimed.

It seems to me that some of the people of Galatia had a similar experience of the presence of Jesus when Paul first preached to them. He describes it like this:

"As you know, it was because of an illness that I first preached the

*gospel to you. Even though my illness was a trial to you, you did not treat me with contempt or scorn. Instead you welcomed me as if I were an angel of God, **as if I were Christ Jesus himself.**"* (Galatians 4:13-14)

Perhaps for the record, I should add at this point that many have also responded to me with utter indifference or outright hatred! But then, I take it that people have always responded to the message of Jesus in these ways too.

I want to stress the importance of personal encounter with Jesus in the lives of His witnesses. As we proclaim His Gospel, we should be filled with His presence and aware of His immediate power to save. Sometimes it seems that we "feel" this more and sometimes less. Of course, we preach in and out of season whatever we feel.

I was speaking in a church once which was very large, but which had virtually no understanding of who Jesus is. I was due to give a talk about the cross one night and as soon as I started to pray in the morning, I saw in my mind's eye an impression of people coming to the front at the end to give their lives to Christ. This was such a strong impression that I felt that I didn't need to pray anymore that day, but just turn up and watch God do what He was going to do.

I gave a presentation about the cross which I have given many times before, but on this occasion I could hardly prevent myself from crying and had to stop several times to regain my composure. I'm not given to crying when I speak, not least because when I do, I don't cry quietly! In fact, many people were crying that night and I made an invitation for those who wanted to respond to Jesus to come forward afterwards. A lot of people came forward and this was the first time in the history of this church of some 4,000 members that anyone had ever made a public response to Jesus in this way. I believe this was a particular work of the Spirit expressing Jesus' compassion for these people, who were trying to follow Him but who did not know Him. I also believe it was an answer to prayer for some who told me that they had been praying that the Gospel would be preached in their church for some fifty years!

This shows how, as empowered witnesses, we can bring the Gospel to people in all its glory, but I believe in order to do this we need to be in touch with the living Jesus ourselves and alive to His immediate presence – because He continues to be the essence of the good news.

4
What is an Evangelist?

There isn't much specific focus on the word "evangelist" in the New Testament. Indeed, it is only used a handful of times. Paul stays at the house of "Phillip the evangelist" in Acts 21:8 and the young Timothy is exhorted to "do the work of an evangelist" in 2 Timothy 4:5. Paul includes "evangelists" as part of the foundational group of leaders seen as the Spirit's gift to the Church (Ephesians 4:11). Of course, this doesn't mean there was little emphasis on evangelism at the time when the New Testament texts were being produced. On the contrary, we can assume that everyone was involved in evangelism judging by the way in which the faith spread so far and so quickly.

So, who were the first evangelists? The obvious answer is the apostles of Jesus. As we have seen, the apostles were a specific group – those who had been with the Lord during His ministry. They were the ones who had been personally commissioned by Him to take the Gospel to the ends of the earth (Matthew 28:16f). Even within the time frame of Jesus' mission, they had been given a trial run at the preaching and healing ministry (Matthew 10:1f). Having been taught and commissioned by Jesus, the apostles were the recognised leaders of the early Church. Together they constituted a leadership group, but even within this group there were leaders of leaders. I am particularly interested in what it means for us to have those who are primarily called and gifted to preach the Gospel as our church leaders.

After the day of Pentecost, evangelistic preaching became the primary focus of the apostles. As the Church grew and the task of distributing food to the poor became more complex, they delegated oversight of this area to others. Things were reorganised so that the apostles would continue to be free to pray and preach the Gospel (Acts 6:1f). Of course, they didn't delegate the running of such a practical task to very suitable people! The naughty Stephen insisted on doing *great wonders and miraculous signs among the people* (Acts 6:8). Which raises the question, where did he find time for the daily distribution of food? This is exactly the sort of thing that happens if you delegate a task to someone *known to be full of the Spirit and wisdom* (Acts 6:3)!

There is scant information about how the apostles set about preaching the Gospel to the whole world, though tradition has it that in the end, they simply cast lots and set off in different directions. And the case of the naughty Stephen points to an ambiguity in the use of the term "apostle" within the New Testament and in the sub-apostolic literature as well. The simple fact is that before very long, new converts became highly anointed and set off to preach the Gospel wherever the Spirit directed them. There soon emerged a roving band of apostolic-evangelists and also prophets who were sometimes sent out and personally supported by churches, and sometimes not. Paul acknowledges this wider group calling them *apostles of the churches* (2 Corinthians 8:23).

This set up a situation which could work out really well, or which could go horribly wrong. On the one hand, you might think there was a good balance to be found in having local leaders of particular congregations and itinerant leaders coming in from time to time.

The former might be responsible for the on-going work of a specific church, but they would be assisted on an occasional basis by the latter who would use their particular gifts to build up the congregation and assist it in its mission for a season. However, these apostolic-evangelists or prophets were sometimes self-appointed and were also the proud possessors of very wrong doctrine which they freely passed on to those they taught. From the Pauline letters it is obvious that such people were the bane of his life (2 Corinthians 11:4f; 1 Timothy 1:3f). In fact, it became difficult to determine exactly who was in charge when they were around and how long they should stay for. The early Church soon felt the need to regulate the relationship between local and itinerant leaders and ministers. The Didache (a first century Christian text) has a surprisingly large amount to say about this. I would trace back to this time the first indications of the difficulty the Church has experienced in relating to its apostolic/evangelists – and vice versa.

How Are Evangelists Different From Other Gifted People?

Paul distinguishes evangelists from apostles, prophets, pastors and teachers in Ephesians 4:11 and it may be worth exploring these distinctions.

Prophets are extremely highly regarded by Paul. Apostles and prophets are linked together in this passage (and elsewhere) and Paul describes prophecy as one of the greater gifts (1 Corinthians 12:31). My own view is that those truly gifted in prophecy have a more vivid experience of the spiritual realm than the rest of us. This makes them appear incomprehensible at times. They often laugh when we weep and weep when we laugh because God's ways are so very different from ours and they are more in touch with them! Imagine that we stand beside the river of spiritual experience including "the depths" of visionary experience, dreams and revelation about what God is

43

doing or is going to do. All who have the Spirit of Christ are splashed by the waters of this experience. We may even go for a paddle from time to time. But real prophets spend a fair amount of time swimming in the river and may find it difficult to dwell for very long on the bank with the rest of us. That's why, for the prophet, everything is more immediate or urgent. Now, apostles are also visionary. Paul speaks of his own revelatory experiences (2 Corinthians 12:1f) and although apostles are not prophets they can at least understand and, more importantly still, interpret what God may be saying through prophets. Apostles drive the mission forward and prophets help to direct their path.

Teachers are not spontaneous bringers of immediate revelation, whose principle concern is with the question: *what is the Spirit saying and doing right now?* Rather they are explainers and interpreters of existing revelation, whose interest is in how we can apply this revelation to our lives in practical terms. Specifically this applies to making clear the truths of the Scripture. Of course, the teaching of God-breathed Scriptures is a prophetic undertaking in general terms and can make an incredible impact, but it is not the same thing as prophecy.

Pastors are concerned with the care and direction of their people. This by no means excludes an openness to the prophetic or an interest in teaching, but I would suggest that in the real pastor, neither of these is the primary focus. A pastor is first and foremost a shepherd to his/her people and has an overriding passion for their well-being and development in Christ.

Evangelists are more specifically announcers of the Good News of Christ. Their calling is to go to those who have not heard and bring them the message. Real evangelists have the power to help people to seal the deal, as opposed to simply bearing witness to a personal experience of Christ, which we are all called to do from time to time. They are also dealing with the given datum of the revelation of Christ and are not therefore the mystical bringers of news about what's currently going on in the heavenly realms. Neither do they have much interest in precise explanations to the Church of complex areas of doctrine, nor are they particularly focused on the needs of people once they are in the Church.

Apostles and evangelists obviously have quite a lot in common. Both convert people, both have to be open to the power of the Spirit, and both break new ground. I believe that apostles have a bias towards establishing and leading new initiatives (like church plants), whereas evangelists are more narrowly focused on the conversion of outsiders. It could be said that apostles are really evangelists that grew up i.e. those who finally developed an interest in the Church or in the churches they create!

Of course, in the first century (and in every century thereafter), the Gospel was also proclaimed by innumerable Christians who would never have taken upon themselves labels like apostle or evangelist. This was (and is) not so much an exercise in formal preaching, but the communication of personal faith to friends and casual acquaintances through natural conversation as believers carry out the activities of their daily lives.

Do Evangelists Have a Personality Type?

I am quite convinced that God uses every conceivable type of Christian person to make the message of the Gospel real. However, God appears to have created us with different personality types and gifts and these are predisposing factors when it comes to identifying how we are to serve in the church and in the world. Of course, we change and life changes too, so I'm not suggesting that some of us are genetically doomed to be evangelists and that we will never do anything else this side of eternity! But I must say that the evangelists

I know do seem to have certain things in common and I think it's useful to examine what they might be.

Let me set this in a broader context. It seems to me that as human beings created in the image of God, we have nothing to lose and everything to gain by trying to accept and understand more fully who God has made us to be. Following on from there, it is equally useful to seek to discover what God has called us to do. I know that some are uncomfortable with this kind of enquiry, believing that it amounts to unhealthy introspection, somehow detracting from the fact that we are new creations in Christ. However, there is surely a distinction to be drawn between self-awareness (which is good) and introspection (which is bad). Although I am a new creation in Christ, this does not mean that I ought to be the same as every other Christian. In fact, I expect to become more the "unique me" as God continues to work in me by His Spirit. So maturity doesn't lie in my seeking to become a bit of everything – apostle, evangelist, pastor, teacher and prophet.

We also badly need to know how to coexist with "aliens". The aliens in question are our brothers and sisters in Christ who have been created differently and who have different callings upon their lives, but who are nevertheless seeking to advance the kingdom of God, just like us. As we know only too well from personal experience, there is nothing like interacting with other people in church to reveal just how challenging is the Pauline call to, *"be completely humble and gentle; and be patient, bearing with one another in love"* (Ephesians 4:2).

Before I began to lead a church, I conducted an exercise in which those of us who were committed to getting things going attempted to establish our fundamental values as a core group. We did this because the church planting material I read (which had been produced by John Wimber) maintained that as a rule, like tends to attracts like. So, if you can identify the fundamental values of the core group in your church, you will know what kind of church you will end up with. I didn't know whether that was true and, if it was, whether I wanted it to be. But a group of about 70 of us set about trying to identify our main values. We sought to get beyond very spiritual answers, such as "like Jesus" who, it seems to me, is more of a person than a value. To help us in this task, we considered questions like this:

1. What motivates me to do what I do most of the time?
2. How would I complete the sentence, "The most important value in my life is…"? Or "I get up out of bed in the morning because of…" (Not the alarm clock)
3. What kind of films would I pay to see?
4. What kind of films would I never watch voluntarily?
5. What kinds of books do I choose?
6. What kind of holidays do I like?
7. What do I like to do with my leisure time?
8. What is my ideal job?
9. What kind of people do I really enjoy being with?

I have now conducted this exercise several times with various groups of Christians (and once with non-Christians) and I have found that people come up with surprisingly similar values which can be divided into three broad categories.

There appear to be people with what I call a strong *adventuring* drive who value such things as risk taking, impact making, stimulation, competition, a sense of humour and intense experience.

There are *carers* who value such things as people, relationships, friendship, community and love.

And there are *truth-tellers* who are interested either in the big picture, the overall vision, the way things work, or in honesty, integrity, justice and responsibility.

I know that we are all meant to express all of these drives and I know that Jesus perfectly embodies them all. However, my experience is that we reflect these drives in different balances and can usually identify more closely with two out of the three. I have noticed that those who have been Christians for a very long time find it genuinely difficult to put themselves in a particular category – but so do those who don't like being put in categories (usually truth-tellers, by the way) and those with little self-awareness.

Let me attempt to identify three "drive profiles" to see if you can identify where you fit into my theory. This is based on what people have frequently said about themselves.

Adventurers

Adventurers value risk taking, impact making, stimulation, passion and freedom. At their best they are visionary, focused, get tasks accomplished, set up new things, are courageous and inspirational to others. At their worst, they pursue their goal at any cost, aren't interested in people except as a means to an end, don't recognise what others are doing, and have their own adventures of which only some are actually worthwhile.

Carers

Carers value love, friendship, community, trust, people-development and long term commitment. At their best, they have a mature understanding of what it means to love people, a commitment to the building of relationships, and are faithful maintainers of long term life-sustaining friendships. At their worst, they are blinded by people's needs and co-dependent with them (they need to be needed), are unwilling to follow a vision if it disturbs the pattern of relationships, and are dependent on the goodwill of those they care for.

Truth-tellers

Truth-tellers value either the big picture (how or why things work) or authenticity, honesty, openness and vulnerability. I distinguish "big picture" from "conscience-driven" truth-tellers, some being more interested in process issues and others with issues of morality. At their best, they are able to show what the truth is in a given situation and thereby save the day and ask essential questions about the process by which something ought to be done. They see to the heart of things and call others to do what is morally right. At their worst, they say the right thing at the wrong time and are rude and destructive with the truth. They can become lost in endless process questions without ever doing anything and miss opportunities as a result. They can lapse into legalism.

Adventurers like projects (this is what I do), carers like to look after people (this is who I am) and truth-tellers like to raise fundamental questions (this is what is right)! I believe that adventurers are apostles and evangelists, carers are pastors, and truth-tellers are prophets or teachers.

One implication of this is that those we need to co-exist in unity with will be those who strongly exhibit drives that we don't. The great challenge of church life, therefore, is how to hold these distinctive and very different drives together in a group of people. I believe that one of the main reasons churches fail to attract people is that they duck out of this challenge. But if we could identify and release diverse expressions of these drives in the life of the church then, theoretically, we would establish churches that everyone would want to go to! Most leaders turn church vision into an expression of the drive/drives that they themselves most embody, and are therefore most comfortable with.

For instance, there are many caring leaders whose communities will never attract outsiders in any number because their only real focus is looking after those who are already in. There are adventuring leaders who create great excitement when they are around, but who are so busy being elsewhere that the church collapses. There are also truth-telling leaders who attempt to set up "pure" churches which are effectively governed by laws and rules usually focused on external behaviour. They don't attract many people either! In fact, I know of one such leader who reduced a church of 800 to 30 over the space of 9 years.

We need a bigger and braver vision than this. Churches need a balanced foundation of leadership upon which innumerable expressions of adventure, care and truth can be built. I am primarily an adventurer, which means that my decisions are always influenced by what I value – risk, impact and outward focus. It is not my job to seek to become someone I'm not, but it is my job to ensure that caring and truth-telling also flourish. It is also my job to stay within the body of the church, despite the internal and external pressures to move on to the next thing.

Apostolic-evangelists have a vital part to play in church life. In fact, I believe that adventurers of this kind should be leading the church supported in their leadership by caring and truth-telling leaders. Adventurers need carers to remind them about the people dimension and truth-tellers to ask about processes and to question whether the adventurer's latest vision is really from God. Carers need adventurers to call them on into a vision and truth-tellers to rebuke their co-dependency. Truth-tellers need adventurers to interpret them and to commit them to courses of action and carers to ask them to please say what they have to say more gently!

So, as I seek to reveal the heart of an apostolic-evangelist with the help of this characteristically Pauline passage (Romans 15:14-20), I would be grateful if you could be asking these questions: *how much of me to do I see in this?* And also, *to what extent do I need to recognise my leadership responsibilities within the church?*

I take Paul to be a classic adventurer. He is a natural leader with an enormous and unique vision whose decision making is revelatory and instinctive and who has an ambivalent relationship with the other apostles (Galatians 2:11f). Someone told me of an interview they'd conducted with an adventurer during which the usual concern about adventurers was expressed: "We aren't sure you are a team player." He responded, "I'm definitely a team player – as long as I'm leading the team." In the life of an adventurer there should be a period of coming into maturity, during which they accept who they are and what they are called to do. After that, serious adventurers should be asked to lead the church or should be thrust out into leadership elsewhere, whilst their church maintains a loose relationship of support with them. Otherwise they will try to take over. As sure as eggs is eggs, adventurers will lead. This is how adventurers tend to, or ought to, function in any church or organisation:

Adventurers are Confident in Their Authority

This has two implications:

a) *They strengthen people through personal affirmation – "I myself am convinced, my brothers, that you yourselves are full of goodness, complete in knowledge and competent to instruct one another"* (Romans 15:14).

A lot of people struggle to believe in themselves. This is less of a problem for adventurers who are often perceived as being arrogant. Adventurers draw on their strong sense of who they are and what they are called to do (usually confirmed in them again and again by Jesus) and they bless from this position of strength. We confirm and bless the wonderful things that God is doing in a situation or in someone's life. I am doing what I do partly because other leaders have been kind enough to bless what God is doing in or through me.

b) *They speak boldly about what is right and wrong – "I have written to you quite boldly on some points, as if to remind you of them again, because of the grace God gave me"* (Romans 15:15). To be more specific, those adventurers who also have a strong truth-telling drive aren't usually backward in coming forward – especially when someone or something is going off track. They have the boldness to say "That's not right" – on the authority of their own conviction, and hopefully God's as well!

Adventurers are Confident in Their Calling

Paul speaks of *"the grace God gave me to be a minister of Jesus Christ to the Gentiles with the priestly duty of proclaiming the gospel of God"* (15:16). Adventurers know where they are going and talk about it a lot. That is because they need other people to go with them. A large vision needs a lot of people with all kinds of skills if it is to be fulfilled. Christian leadership must be revelatory and revelatory leadership attracts people because they sense that God is doing something. The account of the beginnings of David's kingship in the book of Chronicles features several rather dull lists of the people that came to join him – without whom he would never have succeeded.

Adventurers Must Exemplify Humility

Paul says, *"I glory in Christ Jesus in my service to God. I will not venture to speak of anything except what Christ has accomplished through me"* (15:17). Of course, at a popular level, people often think of Paul as lacking in humility – but that is because they have a defective understanding of this virtue. Humility is not the denial of what we are good at; this is the English definition. Humility is the proper appreciation of what belongs to us and what belongs to God. Paul is so confident because he knows that God has called him and that God has commissioned him. It's easy for adventurers to make *themselves* the focus through the force of their own charisma and it is very important that we don't.

Adventurers Demonstrate That What They Say is True

Paul speaks of calling Gentiles to the obedience of the Gospel, *"By what I have said and done – by the power of signs and miracles, through the power of the Spirit"* (15:18-19).

Adventurers have the power to demonstrate the truth of their visions. Signs and wonders confirm that what they say is true. A few years ago now I went to a church in Germany to teach about the work of the Spirit. As I was making my way to the airport, someone on the tube began to spit on my suitcase and take experimental swings with a metal bar, all the while staring at me in a meaningful way. As I left the tube, he took a swing at my head – and missed. It made me think this might be an important trip!

I spoke about the work of the Spirit and about the power of God to heal and then invited the Spirit to come to touch everyone present. There were powerful demonstrations of the Spirit and since that time this church has become a place of refreshment for many people in that part of the country and from further afield. God in His grace was willing to confirm the truth of what I taught by what He did.

Adventurers Break New Ground

Paul says, *"It has been my ambition to preach the gospel where Christ was not known, so that I would not be building on someone else's foundation"* (15:20). Adventurers are innovators, easily bored, needing wide open spaces, enormous challenge and substantially untrammelled freedom if they are to flourish. In spiritual terms, this confidence in Jesus, this authority in His name and power to demonstrate the truth, so often drives adventurers out to new things because they know that what they see in their spiritual imagination is possible.

Where is the battle fought with apostolic-evangelists? We shall look at this question in the next chapter, but in brief, Satan attempts to undermine their confidence in Jesus, compromise their integrity, thwart their calling and inhibit their boldness to demonstrate the truth. Most adventurers get derailed at some stage and from time to time they need fresh encouragement to be who they are, even though they are usually quite strong in this area. They need to grow in their gifts and go on to become the people God has made them to be. Their experiences of inadequacy and failure are often the very things God uses to ensure that the glory goes to Him and not to them, as He fulfils His purposes for their lives.

I worked for three churches before I realised I was gifted to lead. I assumed that because I was less warm and pastoral than many church leaders I had met and admired, I wasn't cut out to lead – indeed, it might be dangerous for people if I did! My first love was preaching the Gospel to non-Christians and my second was teaching about the Spirit. In an ideal world, I liked to do both at the same time. It seemed to me that it would be better if I tried to find a church to which I could be attached as a roving evangelist/speaker.

I now realise that whether I did it well or badly, in fact, I have always attempted to lead. Of course, my leadership has only ever been as effective as I am. Experience counts for so much as does growth into personal maturity. Therefore, an enormous amount of my "leadership" (and I'm looking back over my whole life, not just the period during which I've been a Christian) has been ineffective and rather embarrassing. I fully expect to be embarrassed in years to come when I look back on some of what I take to be good practice now! But, my point is that leaders lead and evangelists often grow into leadership.

So may I conclude this chapter by challenging any evangelist reading it to consider whether you are being prepared to lead? Many churches are led by warm pastoral leaders who are not best suited to the ultimate leadership position. The pastor's heart recoils from growing bigger churches because he knows that he can't give the people the care he feels they deserve. True pastors are not task- but people-orientated and are rarely visionary. Leadership is a task made up of a multitude of tasks and above all else, leaders must have the capacity to receive and impart vision. Evangelists are driven by the task of preaching the Gospel and, if they develop into apostles, by the vision of setting up a multitude of churches through which to fulfil this task.

Therefore, I believe that it is better for churches to be led by apostolic-evangelists assisted by pastors – and not the other way round. Of course, every church needs mature pastoral leaders, and they should be involved at the very heart of church leadership. But pastoral leaders do not exercise the task and visionary aspects of leadership well. Every large church I have seen has been led by a person with a strong sense of vision and outward focus. Perhaps it doesn't matter to God that some churches are small and pastoral in character and some are large and evangelistic. This is the received wisdom. I think it matters to God that all churches are established on the right foundation of gifted individuals – apostles, prophets, evangelists, pastors and teachers.

Paul describes these gifted individuals as the foundation on which any church should be built. If this foundation is not in place, God's people will not be *"prepared for works of service"* (Ephesians 4:12) and will not *"become mature"* (4:13). This is interesting because there is no doubt that the world looks at the Church in England and sees people who are ineffective in what they do and ineffectual in the way they live. I believe that the time has come for us to re-examine what we take to be the foundation of church leadership and for those who are apostolic-evangelists to come in from the cold periphery of the Church and to consider leading from the centre in fulfilment of the biblical mandate.

5
Evangelists and Their Lifestyle

I was converted from abject atheism into a vibrant Pentecostalism. Although I have experienced times of disappointment and pain in my own life, I can honestly say that I have regularly seen demonstrations of the power of God. I attribute this to the sense of expectation both exemplified and encouraged by those who first taught me about the willingness of God to act. From the beginning of my Christian life, I learnt that it was normal to collaborate with God in doing the impossible! I have had the privilege of working in three of the most significant Anglican churches in this country before I began to lead myself. What the leaders of these churches had in common was a determination to be open to the power of God. I have seen that where people seek the power of God's Spirit, there is freedom in the church and also on-going growth.

It seems to me that there are two things we all need to come to terms with in relation to our calling as Christians, but especially as evangelists. One is theological and the other is experiential. Neither of them is easy. I believe that we need to hear these things again and again if we wish to serve God in the power of His Spirit.

1. A theological reality

It is the unmistakable direction of the New Testament that evangelists are called to minister to people or to serve them just as Jesus did. Matthew, in his gospel, makes this painfully obvious. Here is the story of his first ten chapters. Are you ready?

Matthew arranges his material to answer the question "Who is this Jesus?" With Matthew there is no dramatic artifice – he just says it like it is. So, who is He? He is "the Son of David" (1:1), the Christ (1:17). In other words, He is the fulfilment of Jewish Messianic expectations. More than this, He is "Jesus" (the one who saves) (1:21) and finally, He is "Emmanuel" (God with us) (1:23). So Matthew clarifies the question of Jesus' identity right at the beginning of his gospel. He is God the Son, the universal Saviour.

Matthew then calls various witnesses to "testify" that this is true. There are the wise men (2:11), there is John the Baptist (3:11) and there is God Himself (3:17). The divine identity of Jesus – stated by Matthew and backed up by significant witnesses – is then challenged by the devil (4:3).

Jesus proceeds to demonstrate who He is by what He teaches and what He does (4:23). The preaching is found in chapters 5-7 and includes the Sermon on the Mount. The action is described in chapters 8-9 and includes some phenomenal healings. At the conclusion of chapter 9, the main phase of Jesus' ministry is complete. Matthew shows us that He has reached an internal conclusion by the device of repetition (compare 4:23 and 9:35).

Guess what happens next? The focus switches to the disciples (9:36 -10:1). Jesus commits His ministry to them. Maybe this was to be a one-off? No, Matthew presents a very long section known as "the mission discourse" in chapter 10. Why? Because his readership needed to be equipped to continue the itinerant preaching and healing ministry of the Lord. Furthermore, Jesus commits the same ministry to the disciples at the end of the Gospel (28:19). Obviously, they interpret the commission as including healing and the casting out of demons, as Luke makes clear in Acts.

What has the Church done with the Great Commission? We like to observe it but we aren't keen on doing it. *"Teach them to **observe** everything I commanded you,"* says the King James Version. Anglicans in particular like to "observe" things – they set up committees and working parties to do so. We have been so unwilling to "do everything" that we tend to turn the Great Commission into a rather significant Omission. Jesus has committed His ministry to us and our response has been either to domesticate it or to refuse to accept it. We all tend to do one or the other. We have reduced it by seeking to care for needy people in a multitude of practical ways. We have reduced it by wanting to be a loving, non-judgemental presence that wouldn't want to impose any particular views on anyone. We have rejected it on the grounds that modern science discounts the supernatural, or on the basis that the healing ministry was only needed before the emergence of the Holy Bible, which some almost revere in the place of the Holy Spirit.

Actually, this is what Jesus is looking for and this is what the world needs: Christians (and specifically evangelists) who will commit themselves to *all* of that which Jesus commanded us to do. So above all else, evangelists need to become obedient to everything Jesus said. Not just to the loving our neighbour and forgiving people bit, but also to the violent bit. For the Kingdom of God is taken forward by "violent people" (Matthew 11:12). This is the essence of what Jesus did: He preached the Gospel, healed the sick and cast out demons. Evangelists, like all Christians, are called to a multitude of acts of ministry or service. We are to care for people in practical ways and to be salt and light in a hurting world; to be an authentic presence. But above all else, we are called to preach the Gospel, heal the sick and cast out demons. The radical failure of the Church to impact our nation compared with the radical success (not an Anglican word, I know, but I don't see what's wrong with it) of other churches in other parts of the world, is directly related to this disobedience. It is a horrible reality – but it is a reality nonetheless. Churches that are open to the power and ministries of the Spirit grow and those that are not, do not. Evangelists who are open to the power and ministries of the Spirit are far more effective than those who aren't.

Often in the gospels, Jesus seems to do what He does with a breathtaking ease which leads me to the second thing that all Christians and all evangelists need to come to terms with.

2. An experiential reality

If the first reality is that we are called to minister in the same way that Jesus did, the second is the enigmatic nature of our experience of trying to do so.

It should be apparent by now that I really believe in this stuff. In fact, I have been praying for people to be healed or touched by the power of God for 15 years or so. I have travelled around my country and around the world doing so and teaching other people, some of whom have gone on to do the same. However, my experience is enigmatic. For instance, although I have seen the sick healed, although I have cast out demons (and yes, I am aware of the distinction between emotional disorder and the effects of supernatural evil), although I have seen many come to faith through the preaching of the Gospel, there have been times when the last thing I want to do is pray for someone or preach to them. Not because the throng has exhausted me or for some other good reason, but because I'd rather go down the pub and watch the football. I have chosen to do or say things that are in direct contradiction to the Gospel. I have done things that have not brought healing, but hurt. I have prayed for people and known that absolutely nothing was going to happen and, lo, nothing has happened. I have prayed with a great sense of expectation and lo, nothing has happened. When people are healed I find it difficult to believe, even though I do believe. I've seen many people walk away from the challenge of coming to faith. People I've prayed for have died and I've failed to cast demons out of people. I've given into the temptation not to pray for people, but just to say nice things to them instead.

What do you make of this enigmatic "success" story?

I once spent a weekend at a particular church and after one talk offered to pray for any who wanted prayer. A middle aged woman came to the front and told my wife and myself that she had recently had a hysterectomy and asked if we could pray for recovery from the effects of the operation. We invited the Spirit to come upon her and after a while she slid gently to the floor. Shortly after that, we got in the car and set off home. Reflecting on the weekend, I was disappointed because I'd been expecting God to do something spectacular! When I had been praying about the trip the same passage from the Bible kept recurring in several things I read or studied. It was about Paul doing signs and wonders in a particular context. I came to believe that Spirit was telling me that He was going to do something that weekend that would act as a sign of His power in that area, which would help the church to carry forward it's mission there. But nothing like that happened.

A couple of weeks later, I received a remarkable letter from the lady we had prayed for telling me that when she had gone home, her family had realised that her face "looked different". Examining herself in the mirror she discovered that the squint she'd had in her eye since she was a child had been straightened. She had had nine operations to try and correct the squint during the course of her life, none of which had been effective. The squint had caused a problem with acute headaches all her life. Her ophthalmologist could offer no explanation for what had happened. But, of course, we know that God in His grace healed her eye! She gave an account of what had happened to her church and then before the (very liberal) Bishop at some larger meeting. She was interviewed in the local paper and then finally by Woman's Own! And so what God did became a sign and wonder affecting the whole area. But isn't it interesting that my wife and I didn't even pray for the right thing? Enigmatic or what?

So my experience has often been strange even when I'm being effective. And I am not alone. Why is there such a difference between Jesus' experience and our own? With Jesus, it all seems so straightforward. The sick are healed and demons are cast out with a word. The secret lies in some unseen realities in His life which we evangelists need to take on board.

It's like this: I watch a phenomenal gymnastic performance at the Olympics. Someone performs wonders on the parallel bars. I think to myself: "Yes, the parallel bars! Today I will emulate that performance!" In fact, I am about to discover the disparity between my aspirations and my ability. We may feel excited about a lifelong commitment to every dimension of the Great Commission. We may intend to start right now! But to be truly effective over the longer term, some personal building blocks will need to be put in place. We catch a glimpse of these building blocks at the moment of Jesus' baptism (Mathew 3:13-17).

Being obedient

You'd think that Jesus didn't need to be baptised – at least that's exactly what John the Baptist thought. Jesus did it because it was what His Father wanted Him to do, probably as an act of identification with us in our humanity. In the biblical language,

He did it to "fulfil all righteousness". It is well known that Jesus' favourite self-designation was "Son of Man". This title is partly an allusion to the divine Son of Man in Daniel, but it also expresses Jesus' conception of His ministry in terms of suffering service. For instance, we are told that *"the Son of Man did not come to be served but to serve and to give his life as a ransom for many"* (Mark 10:45). The ultimate demonstration of Jesus' determination to choose the will of His Father is seen in Gethsemane.

Once, when I was really struggling with something, a much older Christian listened to my description of what was going on and then said, "Well, that's just you, John." I immediately translated that in my mind, thinking that he meant, "That's just you, John, but of course, you're in the process of being healed in Christ." Actually, what he meant was. "You are who you are and this kind of struggle is typical of someone like you."

As I've gone on in the Christian life, I realise that we don't actually progress from one area of our lives to the next in a systematic and orderly way, as Jesus brings complete healing. In fact, we continue to face the same struggles in specific areas related to our particular damage where Jesus is in the process of healing us. Now and then we find that the struggle is at a deeper level and that more healing is needed. I also realise that the very things I'm good at, or strong in, are the light side of character traits that also have their dark side. For instance, why do so many evangelists fall into sexual sin in particular? Because the ability to bring people to Christ is the light side of a persuasive character trait, the dark side of which is the ability to seduce. Why are evangelists often loose canons who never quite seem to be under anyone's authority? Because the self-determining ability to grasp opportunities for the Gospel is the light side of character traits like boldness and self confidence – the dark side of which is arrogance and self-importance.

I believe that adventuring types often face similar problems. As I suggested in chapter 4, we value risk taking, impact making, stimulation, passion and freedom. At our best, we are visionary, focused, get tasks accomplished, set up new things, are courageous and inspirational to others. At our worst, we pursue our goal at any cost, aren't interested in people except as a means to an end, don't recognise what others are doing, and have our own adventures, of which only some are actually worthwhile.

Therefore, specific areas in which we might seek to be obedient include:

- ensuring that we are involved with other people and other projects
- maintaining significant levels of personal relationship
- recognising that our vision must not always take priority over people-interests
- interacting with those who can question the principles behind what we do

To me this amounts to the call to be a committed and accountable member of a church.

Being loved

I believe that it is very difficult to be used by God unless we are fairly convinced in our hearts that God the Father really loves us. The Son heard these words of affirmation from the Father: *"This is my Son with whom I am well pleased"* (Matthew 3:17; 17:5). The giving out of love is very difficult without a personal experience of love. I have noticed that I am most powerfully used when I have a particular awareness of God's love for me. I hazard the guess that this is because faith is about being able to look confidently into the

Father's face, especially when we pray. We can't do this very well whilst we're harbouring doubts about whether we are really loved by Him. This affects our faith, which affects the movement of God's power through us. It is therefore extremely important that we should be reminded again and again just how much God loves us. Jesus was able to give out compassionate love because He knew Himself to be unconditionally loved.

Being empowered

The Holy Spirit descends on Jesus at His baptism and we shall consider issues of empowerment for service in more detail in chapter 7. However, we should note here that Jesus did nothing whatsoever without the direction of the Spirit.

So Jesus married together obedience in lifestyle and ministry, the receiving and giving of compassionate love and the receiving and giving out of spiritual power in His own life and ministry. Now because we shall never achieve this perfect balance, this could be thought to be discouraging. Our experience of evangelism will always prove enigmatic and we shall always have questions about it, feel we've failed and be tempted to give up from time to time. On the other hand, there is the encouraging reality that Jesus was a human being, just as we are. If He learnt obedience then so can we. If He received the affirmation of His Father then so can we, and if He received the power of the Spirit, then so can we. To become effective in our evangelistic calling we need to grow in these unseen things. We need to grow in our obedience to God, our experience of receiving and giving compassionate love, and in the receiving and giving out of God's power. The more that these building blocks are established in our lives, the more effective we shall be in fulfilling the whole commission of Jesus.

How does Jesus help us to change?

As we read this, I know that some of us will be acutely aware of personal failure in our lives – either concerning something that happened in the past or something that is still going wrong now. We would really like to leave the past behind or to move away from a pattern of behaviour which we know to be wrong, but it feels as if we can't. As a young Christian, I continued to struggle with many patterns of behaviour of this kind and I honestly expected that I would be changed when God decided to zap me! I thought that one day, perhaps through the prayers of an especially anointed person, I would be set free. I came to discover that, in fact, Jesus is always present to us by the power of the Spirit and is able to help us follow Him in every area of our lives – right now! And also that Jesus rarely changes us through a life-transforming zap. We are changed as we learn to walk in His empowering presence.

Shortly after I became a Christian, I was getting ready to go to a party when something suddenly dawned on me. I didn't know how to behave anymore. I knew how I usually behaved at parties. But I sensed (correctly) that a radical change was called for in the light of my conversion. The problem was, I had a desperate need to be found attractive. My identity was inextricably bound up with how women responded to me. To be deprived of the right to elicit a sexual or emotional response from women I found attractive was to be deprived of a large part of my identity. I realise now that I was driven by insecurities about my own masculinity and about whether I would ever find a partner. I had developed a false persona, designed to cover over these insecurities, which I took so deeply into myself that it had become part of my identity.

Many of the problems we face when we come to faith have to do with the radicality of the change involved. The ability to talk about

Jesus doesn't exempt evangelists from feeling the full force of this. We feel either that *we are changing* in radical ways or that our faith *is going to call for radical change* in certain areas of our lives (or both) and we struggle to come to terms with it all, just like any other Christian. Some are acutely aware that, in the light of conversion, they no longer know who they are (I've heard this from recovering alcoholics or occultists), which is frightening. Others are less aware and yet still feel uncomfortable when certain subjects come up, like sex or money or ambition.

Before we consider the change that Jesus brings, it might be worth looking at what makes up our identity, our sense of self or being. It is sometimes taught that we shouldn't delve within – let sleeping dogs lie. There is no reason given in the Bible or from common sense why we should not seek to understand ourselves or find healing from the past. On the other hand, it is possible to delve around so much in the things of the past that we become overwhelmed in the present without resolving what has come up. There can be a failure to move on. Therapy in general has this problem: it is stronger on insight ("Why I am like I am") and weaker on resolution ("How am I going to be any different?") As with many things, there is a balance to be found.

It is generally accepted that our identities are formed by three interrelated influences.

1. *Our heredity:* the characteristics which make us up, derived from our gene pool
2. *Our upbringing:* the social environment in which we grow up
3. *Our culture:* the impact of the corporate values of those around us at national or communal level

For instance, I see that there are precedents for my own struggles with relationships in the lives of my father and grandfather. I see that difficulties I've had with anger and confrontation have a lot to do with the way anger was dealt with when I was growing up. I see that much of the self-confidence that I have benefitted from is because of the hugely affirming quality of my parents' love for me. They always believed in me, therefore I believe in myself. I see that I inherited much of the lower middle class conservatism of my parents. Work hard, be honest, be a good boy, be careful. Like most people of my generation, I recognise that I am suspicious of authority, value the equality of people and the freedom to do what I want to do.

It is an abject mistake to think that we are free-floating individuals, unaffected by our families and peers. In fact, our identities have been moulded and shaped by many influences. Of course, as we grow into maturity we can make certain changes and choices in response to what we have seen and experienced, but I'm not sure that this lifts the weight of all that has gone before. We are who we are – in a sense both with and without Jesus.

The change that conversion brings is so radical that it can only be described in terms of a second birth. Included in that radical transformation is the gift of a whole new identity. Let me trace for you the way in which this gift is given and how it should be received. The process begins with:

1. Identification

God identified Himself unequivocally with His Son, Jesus of Nazareth: *"You are my Son whom I love: with you I am well pleased"* (Mark 1:11). God identifies Himself with any who respond to Jesus, His Son: *"To all who received him, who believed in his name he gave the right to become children of God"* (John 1:12). The identification He makes is relational. We are made to be children of the living God.

God is able to identify Himself with us because of what His Son achieved on the cross and not because of anything in us or about us. Without the cross, God identifies Himself as being separate from us: *"But your iniquities have separated you from your God; your sins have hidden his face from you, so that he will not hear"* (Isaiah 58:2). Nothing in our previous identity either qualifies us or disqualifies us from being accepted by God. No one reading this, I assume, will nurture the conviction that they are too good for God. At this point, we might also abandon the conviction that *we are not good enough for God*. It is an irrational belief, like, if I step on the crack in the pavement, I will go to hell. God does not identify with people because of their goodness but rather on the basis of His grace.

2. Union

Not only are we identified by God – "You are my son/daughter" – but we are also identified with God. In Paul's memorial phrase, we are "in Christ" (e.g. 2 Corinthians 5:17). This has two main consequences:

A) We Have Died

Because Jesus died to sin, so do we. In fact, we die to the entirety of our former way of life. Full immersion baptism graphically symbolises this death when we go down into the waters. It is a physical sign of a spiritual reality. Everything that made up our former way of life has sunk under the waters of death: *"We were therefore buried with him through baptism into death"* (Romans 6:4). So we are now dead to everything by which we would once have defined ourselves outside of Jesus, whether we feel dead or not. Before you became a Christian, how did you identify yourself? As the child of a particular family, as a success, as an athlete, as an intellectual, as go-getter, as a self-made man, as a party animal, as a career woman, as a victim, as an addict, as a failure, as a beauty? The true basis of your identity no longer lies in any of these descriptions. It lies in God's identification of you in relation to Himself. You are a son or daughter of the living God: *"Therefore, if anyone is in Christ, they are a new creation; the old has gone, the new has come!"* (2 Corinthians 5:17) Therefore, abandon here any definition of yourself outside of this relationship – especially if it is a source of pride or pain. Abandon here all identity crises: *"Do you not know that your body is a temple of the Holy Spirit, who is in you, whom you have received from God? You are not your own, you have been bought at a price"* (1 Corinthians 6:19). It is irrational to define yourself according to the dictates of a former way of life, as though you belong to yourself to do with as you wish. Your former way of life has died.

B) We Have Risen

When people come up out of the waters of baptism, it symbolises their emergence into the new, risen life of Jesus. Once again, because we are in Christ, much of what is true of Him is true of us. *"If we have been united with him like this in his death, we will certainly also be with him in his resurrection"* (Romans 6:5). What this means is that we have the power to live out this new identity that God gives to us. What does it mean to be a son or daughter of God? It means we walk in forgiveness, receiving it and releasing it in the power of Jesus. It means that we exercise spiritual authority over evil in the name of Jesus. It means that we are empowered to love, knowing ourselves to be loved. It means we have nothing whatsoever to prove – except the extent of God's love. It means we are free. Ultimately, we shall reign with Christ. He is at the right hand of the Father and we shall exercise authority over the creation under Him. Once again, much of what is true of Him either is or will be true of us.

To be a son or daughter of God is also to have a purpose or purposes: *"For we are God's workmanship created in Christ to do good works which God prepared in advance for us to do."* (Ephesians 2:10). He endows us with spiritual gifts and callings related to our uniqueness, because although we have a common relationship with the Father, He has created us to do different things. Our hearts burn with different passions within the purposes of God. He gives us the power to do everything that He calls us to do and the power to be everything He created us to be. But the sad truth is that Christians often miss out in this area in two main ways.

1. By Trying to Avoid Our Own Death

Sooner or later we have to face the heart of Jesus' invitation: *"Anyone who does not take up his cross and follow me is not worthy of me"* (Matthew 10:38). As the German martyr Dietreich Bonhoffer said, "When Jesus bids a man come and follow him, he bids him come and die."

We can find that although we have come to faith, we do not live from our true identity in Christ. In fact, we carry on as though very little has changed. We still define ourselves according to our old, dead identities. In other words, we continue to nurture aspects of our former lives that go to the heart of who we are – maybe in the relationships, ambitions, or self-understandings that we have. It can come as great news to know that these things need to be seen for what they are – dead. For instance, if you have believed yourself to be worthless, then the news that this identity verdict has been overturned in Christ is incredibly healing – though we still have to choose to receive it. However, if we are talking about a cherished ambition belonging to the former life, then the struggle to lay it down may be intense and painful.

But this is what we signed up for: letting go of our small ambitions and self-understanding etc. When we come to Christ we surrender up to God everything that made up our former way of life. We take up again only that which He allows. This applies especially to those things in which our hearts dwell, since where our hearts are, there our sense of being dwells also. *Christians are actually much happier once they realise they're dead!* Might we catch the great thought that from God comes every good and perfect gift and therefore nothing outside of God is worth having or craving?

Sometimes we attempt to resurrect our dead selves by adding a spiritual veneer to our former identity. For instance, we gain a sense of identity from power, control and status in our former life and simply seek to rediscover those things in the church. In my experience, evangelists have serious tendencies in this direction! Alternatively, we've been used to the attention that comes from being a victim in the world, so now we seek to gain affirmation by being taken care of in the church. If our identity lies outside of our relationship with Him, we shall never be satisfied in Him. We may be an evangelist, a worship leader, the chief flower arranger or the leader of the church, but if these roles become our *raison d'être*, we shall never be satisfied in Christ.

2) By Failing to Live in the Risen Life

Some of us would really like to receive these things, but we feel we don't know how. This may be due to a lack of teaching; it certainly was in my case. If you feel your sense of identity is closely bound up with something from the past, then what do you do? Begin by acknowledging it. Bring it before God when you pray. Recognise who God has now made you to be. You are His child. Ask, "Is this element of my identity something that belongs to my former way of life?" If the answer is "yes", then ask whether it is compatible with being a child of God. Does it need to be re-evaluated? For instance, most of us derive some sense of identity from our families. That is natural. It becomes a problem, however, when the family prides itself on never saying sorry, for example. You would need to die to this family trait. It isn't compatible with being a child of God.

Or, you could collapse your identity into being a mother. It is natural that we define ourselves in part by what God has called us to do. But if the sole focus of our being becomes motherhood then we distort the gift.

We have to relinquish all things back to God, including that which He has given us, otherwise, we become consumed by the gift, distort it and lose sight of the Giver.

Let's say we need to die to something from the past. How do we do it? We recognise that we have been crucified with Christ. We are actually dead to that thing already if we are in Christ. We come in our mind's eye to the cross. We lay it down. We receive by faith the power of the Spirit to live a wholly different life and we choose to forsake that old identity. Then we walk on water. Because it feels like walking on water to behave as Jesus would have us behave. But we fix our eyes upon Him and we begin to walk. On a daily basis, walking in the Spirit has much more to do with this than with hearing God's voice or discerning evil spirits.

I felt God say to me before the party I mentioned earlier, "Just seek to be like my Son." If we seek to be like Jesus, trusting that He empowers us to do so, then we shall be secure in our identities and paradoxically we shall become the very people God intended us to be. This is often a process, especially where we have defined ourselves in a big way by something incompatible with our new identity in Christ. We go back to the fact of our death and to the cross again and again. We receive the power of the Spirit again and again. And we walk in the Spirit again until walking on water begins to feel that little bit more natural.

Sometimes we need the help and counsel of others to make sense of what has gone before and to heal the past. In fact, whenever I've felt God asking me to make a big change, I've needed a special focus of prayer and some measure of advice or support. But the purpose of this support remains the same if it is to be of any use to me: *it has to help me to come to the cross with the wounds of the former life and then learn how to walk away in the power of the Spirit.* Paul says,

"You were taught with regard to your former way of life, to put off your old self which is being corrupted by its deceitful desires, to be made new in the attitude of your minds and to put on the new self, created to be like God in true righteousness and holiness." (Ephesians 4: 22)

6
An Evangelist and His/Her Culture

I attempted to demonstrate in chapter two that the Gospel is fundamentally *good news about the person of Jesus*. In the gospels, the primary content of the news is that the Messiah is here right now! It is generally accepted that there was a widespread interest in the coming of the Kingdom at the time of Jesus amongst His compatriots and Jesus' emphasis upon the Kingdom reflects (amongst other things) His ability to address a distinctive national and religious context appropriately. The good news is first and foremost of the presence or coming of Jesus as Messiah to the historic people of God. The message is brilliantly communicated in word and deed and it makes sense in this specific context.

The first disciples are commissioned to "bear witness" to what they have seen and heard of Jesus in this context. As witnesses, they are called upon to attest accurately "the facts" of the Jesus story. They were there to see the miracles, hear the teaching, mourn the death and hail the resurrection. When the first Christians preached, they obviously weren't claiming to embody the Messiah, but they were announcing that the Messiah had come. Although the disciples believed in the immediate presence of Jesus as they proclaimed Him, they did more than simply declare that He was present! Earlier I wrote that there is an inevitable movement from Jesus as the announcer of news about Himself to the apostles as the announcers of the news about Him. And there is a further movement when the news about Him needs to be communicated in the radically different Gentile context. In this chapter, I want to consider the impact of culture and context upon our proclamation of the Gospel.

Proclamation in a Jewish Context

1. The Pentecost Proclamation

The first task of the Jewish disciples was to demonstrate that Jesus was who He claimed to be to those who had some experience of Him in Israel. Peter's explanation of the extraordinary happenings at the Jewish festival of Pentecost is cast in distinctively Jewish terms. He begins by saying,

"This is what was spoken by the prophet Joel:

'In the last days, God says,
I will pour out my Spirit on all people.
Your sons and daughters will prophesy,
your young men will see visions,
your old men will dream dreams.
Even on my servants both men and women,
I will pour out my Spirit in those days,
And they will prophesy.'" (Acts 2:16-18)

The miracle of speaking in tongues is a fulfilment of the prophetic expectations of ancient Israel. Joel had foreseen that a day would come when God would pour out His Spirit on all flesh. Peter's exposition was similar to what in the Dead Sea Scrolls is called a "pesher" or "interpretation" of an Old Testament text in the light of its fulfilment. So in keeping with the conventions of this Jewish exegetical approach, Peter felt free to change Joel's "afterwards" (as the time when we should expect the Spirit to be poured out) to "in the last days" thereby emphasising that the Spirit's coming has inaugurated the last days. He also applies Joel's word to Jesus so that "the Lord" who brings salvation is no longer Yahweh, caring for survivors on Mount Zion (Joel 2:32), but Jesus who saves all who call on His name (Acts 2:21).

In this context, Peter is in a position to urge national Israel to think again about their personal experience of Jesus of Nazareth. After all, His miracles were performed amongst them (2:22) and they were very involved in His death (2:23). He then referred back to Old Testament Scripture to support the resurrection claim. In Psalm 16:8-11, David clearly wasn't referring to himself when he wrote that God would not abandon Him to the grave or let His holy one see decay (2:27) because his tomb was still in Jerusalem (2:29). All Jews attributed prophetic significance to whatever David wrote and so Peter is able to maintain, *"Seeing what was ahead, he spoke of the resurrection of Christ"* (2:31).

He then moved from Jesus' resurrection to explain His exaltation. It was because Jesus had been exalted that the Spirit had been poured out, resulting in communication about Jesus in a multitude of foreign languages (2:33). Once again the clinching argument was taken from the Old Testament. The ascension of the Christ was foreseen in Psalm 110:

"The Lord said to my Lord: 'Sit at my right hand until I make your enemies a footstool for your feet.'"

David did not himself "ascend to heaven" (2:34) any more than he was preserved from decay. Yet he designated as "my Lord" He whom Yahweh instructed to sit at His right hand. Jesus had applied this verse to Himself (Mark 12:35-37). Peter concluded that "all Israel" should realise that this Jesus whom they rejected and crucified, God had made *"both Lord and Christ"* (2:36).

The proclamation of this message makes an enormous impact on those present: *"Three thousand were added to their number that day"* (2:41). All of which makes it very tempting to think, "Well, all I need to do is to be filled with the Spirit, memorise this argument and then repeat it in the streets of my home town!" But I want to suggest that this proclamation is a perfect example of how to represent the message about Jesus in a culturally relevant way. It is not a timeless blueprint for evangelistic proclamations the world over. Indeed, although I believe in the substantial historicity of the proclamations recorded by Luke in Acts, I'm not sure that he is always purporting to record *everything that was said*, otherwise the apostles were clearly the briefest proclaimers of the Gospel in the history of the Church! I take it that Luke records more *the kinds of things* that were often, if not invariably, said in different contexts. We are told that *"with many other words he warned them"* to repent and believe (2:38). It should be obvious that a religious Jewish context requires Jewish exegetical technique, interaction with Jewish history and prophetic expectation, and a profound familiarity with the scriptures of the Old Testament if our proclamation of the Gospel is to be effective.

Paul employs very similar arguments and techniques in Pisidian Antioch (Acts 13:15f). He is invited to preach whilst worshipping in the synagogue. Addressing both Jews and God-fearers (who would have been familiar with Jewish history and Scripture), he outlines the history of Israel. Here the focus is on the promise of a descendant from David (13:22-23). Then he bears witness to the death and resurrection of Jesus with reference to the fulfilment of Psalm 2:7,

Isaiah 55:3 and Psalm 16:10. We should take it that such was the general pattern when the apostles preached to Jews.

I have always found the ancestral lists in various books of the Bible to be extremely tedious, but I am not surprised to discover that they are still of utmost interest to those who come from a Jewish background. In the same way, I fear that I would have found it rather hard to stay awake during Stephen's presentation of the Gospel to the Sanhedrin (Acts 7:1-53). Once again, it is a recitation of the whole history of Israel with particular reference to the inability of God's historic people to do what He wanted them to do. But, as a Gentile, what has that got to do with me? I do know that I have been unnaturally grafted into the true vine and that this history is now my history in a spiritual sense. But it still doesn't appeal to me and certainly wouldn't have done before I was converted.

The point is that I don't think that addresses of this kind were ever meant to appeal to people from my context and neither were they meant to be taken as universal blueprints for the proclamation of the Gospel. I'm glad that the Sanhedrin got the point though!

Proclamation in a Gentile Context

We have two instances of the sorts of things that Paul said when he preached to Gentiles. The first arises out of a visit to Lystra, which was one of the regions into which the Roman province of Galatia was divided. It appears that the local Lycaonians were largely uneducated and illiterate. However, they were well aware of an ancient local legend in which Zeus and his son Hermes once visited the hill country of Phrygia disguised as human beings.

Apparently, they sought hospitality from local mortals but were rebuffed again and again. Eventually they found a poor couple who were willing to take them in and they were later rewarded by the gods, whilst the inhospitable were destroyed. Stone altars have been discovered near Lystra which indicate that Zeus and Hermes were worshipped there together.

So when Paul performs an astonishing miracle of healing they leap to the obvious conclusion:

"In Lystra there sat a man who was lame from birth and had never walked. He listened to Paul as he was speaking. Paul looked directly at him, saw that he had faith to be healed and called out, 'Stand up on your feet!' At that the man jumped up and began to walk." (Acts 14:8-10)

The Lycaonians believe (not unnaturally) that they have been favoured with another divine visitation and they begin to start making sacrifices in honour of the gods (14:11-13). I think it might be worth underlining what Paul says to them in full once he recovered from the shock:

"We are bringing you good news, telling you to turn from these worthless things to the living God, who made heaven and earth and sea and everything in them. In the past, he let all nations go their own way. Yet he has not left himself without testimony: he has shown his kindness by giving you rain from heaven and crops in their seasons; he provides you with plenty of food and fills your hearts with joy." (14:15-18)

When we read the account of Paul's preaching to the Jews in Antioch, we are immediately thrust into the world of the Old Testament, its history, prophecies and law. Although our present passage is very brief and is no doubt only suggestive of Paul's approach to proclamation in a Gentile context, it should be noted that it contains not one reference to Jewish history or Scripture. Evangelists not working in a Jewish context should therefore take careful note of the following Pauline ingredients when we are seeking to proclaim the Gospel to Gentiles!

1) God is the Creator

Most people believe in God, including many who would never choose to go to church or identify themselves as Christians. The staggering complexity of the universe juxtaposed with what appears to be a minute attention to detail continues to cause most to believe in a Creator. Isaac Newton once suggested that in the absence of any other evidence for the existence of God, the way in which our thumbs work would be enough for him! This is a fruitful first base because, although many believe in God as Creator, they do not claim to know much more about Him other than the fact that He created the world. Is He a gas or an impersonal mass? Is He in everything or detached from His creation altogether? We are able to say, "The Creator God has come as close as hands and feet and as near as breathing. Let me tell you about Jesus."

2) God is Good

Those who believe in God also tend to believe that He is good (Allah is ambiguous in this respect). Paul affirms that the living God, by whose power he has just healed someone, is the very One who provides everything the Lycaonians need to enjoy life. Who wants to believe in a god who has basically got it in for them? Again, we are able to affirm, "The God you experience as Provider has actually provided for us more fully than you can imagine. Let me tell you about Jesus."

3) You Have a Knowledge or a Sense of God

That we believe in God as Creator and sense that He must be for us and not against us, reflects the fact that we have been created by Him and this effectively constitutes our "knowledge" of God. Why (especially in the West) do people blame God when they suffer? Because they presuppose that He created the world and that He is good – which is probably reflective of the last traces of the Western Christian heritage. Suffering isn't a problem unless we believe in a benevolent God. Catholic theology has tended to stress a continuum in our knowledge of God, of which this belief in God as Creator is the starting point and faith in Jesus is the culmination.

Others argue that a sharp distinction should be drawn between what we can know of God by "natural revelation" and what we can know of God by faith in His Son. Paul appears to suggest elsewhere that what we know of God apart from Christ is only useful in that it condemns us (Romans 1:18-19). I believe that we can hold these two ideas together. We can affirm that there is no complete knowledge of God outside of Christ, and also that it is possible for us to know *something* of the One who has made us prior to conversion, and even that some people (though not most) are remarkably true to what they do know. This enables us to say, "You will almost certainly be aware of the One we are talking about in your own experience. The wonderful thing is that it is possible to know Him more fully. Let me tell you about Jesus."

4) You Are Worshipping Something Other Than God

Whether or not people believe in God, there is no one who does not worship. We fill our lives with all manner of meanings. There are a small number who even attempt to live their lives as though everything is meaningless. We give meaning or attribute value to certain things in our lives. Those things might include a set of moral or cultural beliefs and they might embrace specific people we care for. The vast majority do set people, ambitions or beliefs at the centre of their lives. In other words, they devote themselves to these things and are therefore worshippers of them. For instance, worship is seen amongst lovers, football supporters, investors and parents. We are in a position to appeal to the common experience of emptiness that comes when people worship anything less than God. We can say, "We too know what it is to have set ourselves at the centre of the universe and to have found that it doesn't fully satisfy. But it doesn't have to be like that. Let me tell you about Jesus."

So in proclaiming Jesus to Jews, the common ground is our spiritual heritage, the Old Testament and the experience of national Israel. In proclaiming to Gentiles, the common ground is our human experience: we are believers in the Creator, who know in our hearts that He is good, and that we have been created to worship Him.

The same themes emerge from the distillation of Paul's preaching in Athens (Acts 17:16f). Although he was appalled by this city "full of idols" Paul must also have been exhilarated by the openness of the Athenians to the discussion of new ideas (Acts 17:18-21). What an opportunity! He begins by agreeing with them that God is the Creator. It is He who has *"made the world and everything in it, the Lord of heaven and earth"* (17:24). We cannot exist without Him, indeed *"in him we live and move and have our being"* (17:28). Paul even exploits the intimate relational language of one of their own poets: *"We are his offspring"* (17:28b). However, though they have a common belief in God as Creator, Paul has come to make known to them the One they search after. He says,

"I see that in every way you are very religious. For as I walked around and looked carefully at your objects of worship, I even found an altar with this inscription: 'to an unknown god.' Now what you worship as something unknown, I am going to proclaim to you." (17:22-23)

Paul strongly emphasises the goodness of God here as well. It is he who *"gives all men life and breath and everything else"* (17:25), *"determined the times set for them and the exact places where they should live"* (17:26), and *"is not far from each one of us"* (17:27). The Athenians know God as Creator and they know of His goodness; indeed some of them even regard themselves as His offspring (17:28). However, they are not worshipping Him aright for *"he is not served by human hands as if he needed anything because he himself gives all men life and breath and everything else"* (17:25).

Paul is purporting to be in a position to correct their view of God and their experience of worship. Why should they listen to this foreigner? Because he's claiming to have had a personal encounter with someone who came back from the dead. Someone coming back from the dead is the kind of news that transcends any culture! Everyone everywhere knows that everybody dies and that no one comes back. If someone has come back from the dead then we all have to listen to the One to whom it happened, no matter what our cultural context. Paul maintains that although Jesus may have ministered and died in Israel, He is shown to be the universal Saviour by His resurrection from the dead. He declares that God, *"has set a day when he will judge the world with justice by the man he has appointed. He has given proof of this to all men by raising him from the dead"* (17:31).

So, in our proclamation of the Gospel in a Gentile context, we establish common ground by appealing to a belief in, and some experience of, a good Creator. We challenge our hearers to worship the living God and nothing less than Him; and we stake our claim to be right in what we say on the basis of the resurrection of Jesus.

For some years now I have been giving the following summary of the message of Jesus near the beginning of every Alpha course I lead. When addressing the question, "Who is Jesus?" I suggest that His central message can be summarised in four statements:

1. Human life will always lack ultimate meaning unless Jesus lives at the centre of it
2. It is our self-focused refusal to surrender the control of our lives into His hands that separates us from God the Father who has made us
3. But the selfless death of God the Son in our place at the cross has put an end to that separation for any who will receive Him into their lives
4. Jesus offers relationship in the power of His Spirit in exchange for a recognition of the futility of putting ourselves at the centre of the universe

It should be obvious that this is miles away from the language of repentance, Messiah or Kingdom. It is miles away from arguments about David's tomb, Joel's prophesies or the fulfilment of the Law. That, as we have seen, is the language and content of proclamation to the Jews and we have to ask ourselves the question: *how much of my presentation of the Gospel really applies to my context?* In our zeal to be true to the Gospel, we should not underestimate how brilliantly Jesus and His first Jewish disciples fashioned the message, so that it could be heard by the people of Israel. We should not underestimate how hard we need to work to communicate half as brilliantly in our own culture.

Jesus, Israel and the Preaching of the Gospel

Contemporary New Testament theologians have been entirely correct in criticising the traditional Protestant characterisation of Israel as a people who believed that they maintained a right relationship with God by the correct performance of religious duties. The Reformers interpreted Paul's teaching about "works of the law" (in Romans and Galatians) as an invective against an attempt on the part of the Jews to "justify" themselves in this way. They believed that the Catholic Church of their day was guilty of doing precisely this.

In fact, the people of Israel always knew that their status as God's people was a gift of God's grace, having to do with His extraordinary generosity and not their religious performance. The expression "works of the law" seems to be better understood as a term denoting circumcision and observance of food laws as badges of membership in national Israel. Paul's point is that merely being born a Jew *without being one inwardly* is not, and never has been, enough to justify a person before God (Romans 2:28-29, 4:1-8).

The most radical thing Paul taught is that, in the light of the new thing that God has done in Christ, membership of national Israel does not make you part of the people of God. Of course, this has implications for what we teach Christians who join our churches today. Do we continue to encourage tithing, Sabbath observance and beating children because they are in the Old Testament? *It also has major implications for how we preach the Gospel today.*

We should not treat a contemporary Gentile as though he is actually a first century Palestinian Jew! Why do people hand out tracts or wear billboards with passages from the King James version of the Bible firmly affixed? Why do people spend a lot of money taking out advertising space in the underground system in central London with similar messages in the same language? Because they are trying to be true to what they take to be the biblical model of proclamation. I suggest that much of the language and many of the concepts expressed in these things belong to a first century Jewish context. I hazard the opinion that a message like, "Repent for the Kingdom of Heaven is at hand" would mean virtually nothing to a Gentile – ancient or modern!

We need to take very seriously indeed the historic particularity of Jesus' ministry in Israel and that of the mission of the early Church in Israel. I hope that our examination of Paul's preaching in Gentile contexts shows that he did. The very reason why Paul got into so much trouble with the church of Jerusalem and with "the Judaizers" was that he drew the logical conclusions from Jesus' ministry that membership of the people of God no longer has anything to do with badges of national identity. It has to do with faith in Jesus and nothing else. There are many implications of this, but one is that we do not have to stay loyal to the language and religious categories of first century Judaism when we preach the Gospel in our different cultures today. In fact, it is a mistake if we do.

Obviously, our faith in Jesus is not the place to *start* when it comes to a dialogue with Jews or Gentiles. With religious Jews, the starting place would be our common spiritual tradition and with Gentiles it would be our common experience of life. That's why car stickers like, "Thank God for Jesus" or church notice boards like, "Carpenter from Nazareth seeks joiners" or (may the Lord forgive whoever invented this one) "Jesus isn't just for Christmas, He's for life" are such a total waste of time, space and money! What would be of more use in a large city would be a photo of a businessman in rush hour, or working late at the office, with the strap line, "This is the life! Isn't it?" which ironically keys into a whole series of questions that point to the fact that this isn't really "the life" at all.

The Judaizers who appear in the New Testament were Christians who wanted things to stay as they were. To be sure, there needed to be faith in Jesus, but they believed that there also needed to be a strict adherence to cultural and religious Judaism. This reflects the common human tendency, not confined to the Jews of Paul's day, to attempt to keep on doing it like we've always done. I think of the Salvation Army who, at their foundation over a hundred years ago, set Christian words to contemporary pub songs, thereby making the Gospel immediately accessible. The trouble is, they're still singing them today. I think of the Methodists who established a circuit so that their apostolic leaders could oversee several congregations at a time of great growth in the eighteenth century. The trouble is, they're still stuck with the same system. I think of those who feel they haven't done communion properly unless they use a service form dating from centuries ago, written in language that isn't used by them (let alone anyone else) at any other time in their daily lives. The trouble is, it doesn't matter to them that no one else can understand or feel at home with it.

And this same tendency is in me too. I am sometimes brought face to face with this when people suggest we do things differently! I have found myself wanting to say, "But this is how we do it here!" I remember receiving a letter from someone who was converted in dramatic style and had been attending the church for three weeks. Over that period, she'd got used to the songs and wrote a detailed case for continuing to use them after she'd attended a service during which several new songs were sung!

I believe that the Church in this country continues to be ineffective because it does not take its various cultural contexts seriously. We aren't adequately reflecting back to the culture the stories that are currently being told about life at work, in pubs, homes and clubs, and we aren't applying properly to these stories the transforming story of Jesus. I will attempt to consider how we might do so in our preaching in chapter eight.

7
An Evangelist and the Spirit

We may have worked out how to explain our conversion and how to present the Gospel in terms appropriate to our culture; we may have studied preaching techniques and be seeking to live as salt and light in the world. But, without the power of the Spirit we will never be effective evangelists. More than this, without the power of the Spirit we shall never live fruitful Christian lives. As we have seen, the Gospel is the proclamation of Jesus Christ – both who He is and what He has done for us. However, the Holy Spirit is the person in whose dimension of life we experience God. Therefore, without Him we have nothing.

It might be worth pointing out that the Holy Spirit is neither a special atmosphere nor a spooky feeling that comes over us when we sense that we are close to God. He is not a free floating power like electricity. He certainly is not reducible to the Scripture any more than the totality of an artist's being is reducible to one of his paintings. He is the third person of the Trinity and there is no more reason to be cautious or conservative in our attitude to His work than there is to be cautious about the work of the Father or the Son. To say, as one woman is reputed to have done, "Vicar, I hope that *nothing supernatural* will happen in this church" is the same as saying, "Vicar, I have *no idea* what Christianity is!" The Holy Spirit, who wants to interpenetrate the entirety of our being, *is the indispensable necessity of the Christian life* – let alone the evangelistic commission of Jesus. We cannot hope to preach Jesus unless we are empowered by the Spirit of Jesus.

The Holy Spirit in the Old Testament

In the earliest strata of the biblical material, we see God progressively revealing Himself to specific people. As they experience and begin to seek Him, their understanding of God grows. This process starts with Abram who presumably worshipped the supreme god El in ancient Mesopotamian pantheon before being called by the living, yet unknown, God to leave everything and follow (Genesis 12:1). It is possible that this same call came to Abram's father who did not respond. Therefore, from the beginning, the most important thing about Abram is that he does. His responsiveness to God enables the relationship to develop. However, he continues to call God El or IL because he knows of no other name for God. As God reveals things about Himself to Abram, Abram gives him little descriptive epithets like *El Shaddai* – "He is the God who provides". It isn't until the time of Moses that the people of God discover His name, which turns out to be the somewhat enigmatic: *"I am who I am"* (Exodus 3:14).

The point is that God is happy to disclose Himself to those who begin to seek Him and it doesn't seem to matter to God that this disclosing process starts small and takes time. In our human experience, all worthwhile relationships take time. If we are to understand the Bible (and the work of the Spirit in the Bible) we have to take seriously this idea of a progressive revelation or disclosure on God's part concerning His identity and activity in the world.

There are so many standard aspects of the Christian faith that simply aren't developed in the Old Testament. Occasionally, someone like David speculates about a future for the relationship between God and His faithful servants beyond death. It was generally thought, though, that when people died they continued an existence of sorts in *Sheol* – a nether world in which people became rather like cars without working batteries. But God is known to be the God of the living and not the dead and there is hardly a glimpse of resurrection in the Old Testament. God hadn't revealed that yet.

Also, the writers of the Old Testament have a very marked stress on the sovereignty of God – to such an extent that God is effectively described by Isaiah to be the author of good and evil (Isaiah 45:6f). It is, of course, a major revelation to understand that there is but one God who is over all things. But there is a parallel (though limited) development in understanding within the Old Testament about the role of supernatural evil in the shaping of events. We can trace a development in understanding, as theologians in the Old Testament try to hold together the sovereignty of God and the existence of evil. But we start from a position in which evil is also from God. For instance, in the early account of the tormenting of Saul in 1 Samuel 16:14, the spirit that comes to him is "from the Lord". However, in overall terms, there is comparatively little in the Old Testament about the identity and role of "the Satan".

In the same way, the picture of the work of the Spirit that emerges in the Old Testament is shadowy or enigmatic. There is much that is not revealed. Certainly, His presence designates the very presence of God in power and is therefore a mark of His favour. For instance, Gideon may be the least of His people, but when the Spirit of the Lord comes upon him he is able to do extraordinary things (Judges 6:34).

But, throughout the Old Testament, we see the problem of what I think of as "unmediated God". Why did Uzzah die when he reached out to steady the ark? Because he did the wrong thing to a holy thing (2 Samuel 6:6-7, Numbers 4:15, 29-33). Why wasn't Moses allowed to enter the promised land, although he was the meekest man that ever lived? Because he struck the rock when he should have spoken to it. He did the wrong thing with that very holy thing – the power of God.

This underlines the fact that when the power of the Lord is present in the Old Testament to accomplish His purposes, the obedience of the people of God has to be perfect. And, of course, that proved to be rather difficult. There were no perfect people then either – not one prophet, king or leader. Therefore, a very small number of people in the Old Testament were anointed by the Spirit and remained so, until they blew it. There is virtually no *mediation* in the Old Testament between the God of all holiness and His fallen creation. This is part of the problem of unmediated God: the Spirit of the Lord cannot continue to rest upon the unholy. The other part of the problem is that without mediation, God must destroy all that is unholy.

This is the logic of holiness or justice: it must destroy that which is unholy or unjust. Would we not seek to prevent someone abusing a child? That is the divine sense of holiness or justice at work in us because we are made in His image. The logic of holiness or justice is that it seeks to overcome and obliterate that which is unholy or unjust. This explains why people in the Old Testament expected to die if there was a possibility that they might have to see the Lord face to face (Judges 6 22-23). They could not expect God to look upon them without destroying them because of their sinfulness.

So, in the Old Testament, the Spirit is poured out on particular people at particular times and for particular purposes. And He generally remains with them until those purposes are fulfilled, or until they fail. This is painfully true of Saul. It is even true of the great prophet Elijah, who did such amazing things by the power of the Spirit, but who ultimately ran away from Jezebel and had his commission withdrawn (1 Kings 19:15-16). All these are exceptional heroes of the faith in that *they managed to follow the Spirit at all*. It is hardly surprising that in the end, the problem of unmediated God caught up with each one of them.

The Holy Spirit in the New Testament

A much fuller picture of the Holy Spirit emerges in the New Testament. First of all, He is everywhere in the texts! At the very start of Luke's Gospel, we discover that John the Baptist *"will be filled with the Holy Spirit even from birth"* (Luke 1:15), that *"The Holy Spirit will come upon"* Mary (Luke 1:35) and that the pregnant Elizabeth *"was filled with the Holy Spirit"* when Mary comes to visit her (Luke 1:41). At Jesus' baptism, *"the Holy Spirit descended on him in bodily form like a dove"* (Luke 3:22) and immediately thereafter He is led out by the Holy Spirit into the wilderness (Luke 4:1). Luke and Acts go on to be filled with the explosive activity of the Spirit.

Of course, Jesus did not begin His ministry until after His baptism. It appears that the Spirit had not been poured out upon the incarnate Son until that moment. There is, of course, endless theological debate about what it means to say that the eternal Son came to dwell amongst us in human form! I am of the opinion that it means, amongst other things, that the Son voluntarily laid aside various divine attributes – like omniscience and omnipresence. As mentioned earlier, I also believe that Jesus *came to understand* who He was as He grew into adulthood – not least by His reflection on the Scriptures of the Old Testament. Not that God "adopted" Him as a representative human, but that although He always was who He was, in becoming a human and then developing as one, He had to come to realise who He was.

If I am correct in my assumption, then Jesus did no mighty works prior to His baptism because He had no power to do them. It was only after His baptism, when the Spirit descended upon Him, that the action could begin. It is explicitly stated that Jesus both entered and returned from the desert, *"full of the power of the Spirit"* (Luke 4:1,14). In other words, once the Spirit had been poured out upon Him, He continued to remain with Him, no matter what happened. But until the Spirit was poured out upon Him, there was no power for ministry.

As we have seen, Jesus believed that He was able to fulfil His Messianic calling because the Spirit of the Lord was upon Him and He went on to heal the sick, cast out demons and perform nature miracles by the power of the Spirit. It seems to me that Jesus was utterly dependent on the power of the Spirit in every dimension of His ministry. In other words, I don't believe that Jesus simply "Godded" people – because He was God the Son, He just knew what to do and had the power to do it! His power to minister did not come from His identity as God the Son, because He was at that time God the Son *incarnate in human flesh*. It came from the obedient dependency of the incarnate Son on the power of God the Spirit and the direction of God the Father. This is why He says, *"I tell you the truth, the Son can do nothing by himself; he can only do what he sees his Father doing"* (John 5:19) or still more starkly, *"By myself, I can do nothing"* (John 5:30).

We need to come to terms with the reality of the incarnate Son's utter dependency upon the Father and the Spirit because it gives us something in common with Jesus. In ourselves, we are utterly powerless too. Of course, there is a distinction between Jesus in human form and any other human – the little matter of His moral perfection and our limitations in the morality department. But when it comes to fulfilling our calling (including our calling to preach the Gospel) we share with Jesus the need to be totally dependent on the Spirit.

The Promise of the Spirit

It should be borne in mind that at the time when the gospels were being written many of Jesus' first disciples were alive and operating as leaders in the early Church. The candour of the authors of the gospels in describing their general dullness or abject failure speaks enormously for the authenticity of the accounts. The gap between what Jesus is trying to communicate and what they actually understand sometimes reaches tragi-comic proportions. I think especially of the build up to the raising of Lazarus in John's Gospel, where Jesus is trying to explain to them what He is about to do. The disciples are so wide of the mark that they actually think they are being presented with an opportunity to die themselves (John 11:16). Naturally, when they are actually presented with this opportunity at the arrest in the Garden, there are no takers! This lack of comprehension on their part isn't really surprising. No one finds it easy to hear what they don't want to hear and no one finds it easy to hear some aspects of the call to discipleship. And also, more significantly, much of what Jesus says cannot be understood without the help of the Spirit!

At the peak of Jesus' ministry, the disciples must have wondered what they had done to deserve the privilege of having Him as an intimate companion and of seeing incredible miracles on a daily basis. They must have been stunned when Jesus appeared to be sending *them* out to preach the very same message of the Kingdom and exercise the very same power in His name (Matthew 10:1). Especially when He made it clear that their first mission trip would be a) without Him and b) without, *"any gold, silver or copper in your belts"* and c) that they should also leave behind, *"a bag for the journey, or extra tunic, or sandals or a staff"* (Matthew 10:10). But this must have paled into insignificance compared with the shock of being told by Jesus that He was going to Jerusalem and that there He would die (Mark 8:31). And, at the Last Supper, that *it would actually be good for them* that He was going (John 16:7). Jesus meant, of course, that *the way by which He would go* (via the cross and resurrection) would make possible a whole new dimension of relationship and understanding, and that this would be incredibly good for everyone. Jesus tells them that His going will enable the Counsellor to come (16:7) and that there is much more for them to know – more than they can presently cope with, *"But when he comes, he will guide you into all truth"* (John 16:13). They must have felt very disturbed and confused.

The Day of Pentecost

But their confusion turns to horror and then, after three days, to uncontainable joy. On the day of Pentecost, the disciples are continuing to wait for Jesus to fulfil His promise and pour out the gift of the Spirit upon them (Acts 1:4). In order to understand the true significance of what happened we have to go back to the problem of unmediated God.

If an artist produces a painting, does he merge with the painting so that to know the painting is to know him? If an author writes a book, does he merge with what he has written so that to know the book is to know him? Ultimately, there is more to a person than what they create, even if what they create expresses something about them. The creator always remains distinct from his/her creation.

When we proclaim that God created the world, we are not saying that God and His creation are one. God is wholly other than, or distinct from, what He has made – even if what He has made reveals something about Him. This is why it is foolish to search for the god within ourselves, for God is wholly other than us, even though we are made in His image.

Neither may we reduce God to our "highest" human experience – the experience of love. Human love is no more or less than a gift from the Creator given to enrich our experience as His creatures. Although the Bible teaches that *God is love*, our imperfect and highly personalised experiences and definitions of love do not encapsulate the totality of the Creator Himself. In the same way, although some Christians teach this, we do not actually touch Jesus when we touch the poor. As a person in His own right, Jesus is wholly distinct from any part of this creation, even a part He especially loves.

Imagine that you owned every painting by a particular artist or every book by a specific author; that you had longed to know them not just through deep reflection on their work, but to know them through personal experience. Imagine that one day you meet them and that, miraculously, a friendship forms so your knowledge of them is no longer limited to the study of what they have made, but is now also *direct and unmediated* – personal to you.

This is what happened at Pentecost. God, who is wholly other than us, found a way of coming as close as possible. No longer do we need to guess at God by gazing upon what He has made or by searching for a dim reflection of Him within ourselves. *Now it is possible to encounter Him personally.* The way by which Jesus leaves His disciples (via the cross and the resurrection) resolves the problem of unmediated God. Authentic relationship between the all-Holy God and His fallen creatures is made possible through the cross. From the high heart of heaven came the burning lover's Son, throwing wide His arms in welcome to us living, disappearing ones. At the cross, God reconciles a vital aspect of His otherness (His holiness) with our sinfulness, the disparity between the two being the great source of tension within God throughout the Old Testament. At a theological level, Pentecost is the culmination of the great story of how God, who is distinct from us and wholly other than us, has nevertheless found a way of interpenetrating those who look to the Son by His Spirit.

At a personal level, Pentecost is about being loved by God and about delighting in His love. Whenever I consider the familiar story in Acts 2:1f of the coming of the Spirit upon the disciples, I notice that their experience is absolutely overwhelming. The presence of the Spirit affects all their senses, intoxicating them (2:2-4). The only reason some of the onlookers accused them of being drunk, although it was only nine in the morning, was that they appeared to be behaving like drunkards (2:13). It is as if they have been ravished! The angelic realm scoops up the fallen earth and kisses it on the lips! The disciples are left staggering and stammering – speaking in tongues. In other words, they are given other words by which to express the possibility of intimate communion with the God who has come near and, of course, it has to be described as the language of angels! The disciples are transformed in that moment from mere believers into ecstatic lovers.

The disciples are also empowered to be witnesses. Just as with Jesus, they do no works of power until after this empowering moment. Thereafter, the action begins in earnest and they follow the model of Jesus. They are bold and fearless in proclaiming the Gospel (Acts 2:14f, 3:11f and 4:8). They perform remarkable acts of power (2:41, 3:5f, 5:12f). Even nature miracles are included in their ministry (12:1f).

The centrality of the Spirit to the Christian life

Much of this will be familiar, but it might be worth underlining the centrality of the work of the Spirit in the Christian life according to the New Testament:

1. No one comes to faith without the work of the Spirit (John 3:5)
2. God makes His home in us by His Spirit (1 Corinthians 6:19)
3. We are changed into the likeness of Christ by the Spirit

(2 Corinthians 3:18)

4. We hold together as the family of God by the Spirit (1 Corinthians 12:13)

5. We live out the Christian life in the power of the Spirit (Galatians 5:25)

6. We are gifted in our different ways by the Spirit (1 Corinthians 12:7f)

7. We exercise our gifts in the power of the Spirit (Acts 6:3)

8. We pray with the help of the Spirit (Romans 8:26)

9. We are told to go on being filled with the Spirit (Ephesians 5:18)

From this I deduce that there isn't very much about Christianity that doesn't involve the Spirit! So it is impossible to think about evangelising without thinking about the Holy Spirit. If we are to be effective in our preaching of the Gospel, we must be people of the Spirit i.e. those who are immersed in the life of the Spirit, anointed by the Spirit, and dependent on the Spirit in what we say and do just as Jesus was.

Has anything happened to suggest that the *modus operandi* for effective evangelism has changed from the model we find in the ministry of Jesus and that of His disciples? Is there anything in the New Testament to suggest that Spirit-empowered preaching is no longer necessary to evangelism? Is there anything in the New Testament to suggest we should no longer expect the Spirit empowered-preaching of the Gospel to be accompanied by signs and wonders? Let's imagine we were to take a new convert and lock him in a room until he'd read the whole New Testament! What if we were to ask him to write down a summary of what he thought Christians should do based on his reading? Surely, he'd never come up with the idea that we shouldn't expect God to work in miraculous ways anymore!

On what basis could the commands to love God and our neighbour continue to apply beyond the "apostolic period" whilst the commands to heal and cast out demons do not? Some Christians (like some atheists) seem to rely on arguments from experience and not from Scripture: *"I don't experience the power of the Spirit in miraculous ways, therefore He does not work in miraculous ways..."* or *"I've* heard of this flaky story about miraculous claims, so we ought to be terribly cautious about these things..." In fact, there are innumerable accounts of healings in the name of Jesus from around the world (including many that have been medically verified) and of most, if not all, of the rest of the miracles described in the New Testament. To suggest that "these things don't happen" is simply a denial of reality.

But, more importantly, that God performs miracles is a constant theme running throughout the whole Bible. God didn't even think that the drama of Acts 2 was enough for the disciples! A similar thing happens in Acts 4. Didn't God realise that this might cause the disciples to develop a theology based on their experience? There is nothing in the New Testament to suggest that we ought to draw a distinction between preaching (that's still OK) and healing (that isn't) when it comes to evangelism. Miracles point to Jesus and help people believe; preaching explains about Jesus and helps people believe. I'm sure that when the time came to release the young convert from his room and his reading he would proclaim with joy, "It's all wonderfully straightforward: God is alive and He is powerfully at work to ensure that the Gospel goes to the ends of the earth!"

The Spirit and the Evangelist

Jesus needed to be empowered by the Spirit before He began His ministry and so did His disciples. Clearly then, we also need to be empowered by the Spirit to preach the Gospel. The stories of many of the best known evangelists in Church history reach a decisive turning point after they have been empowered by the Spirit. I'm not going to rehearse these now, but it is well worth reading about the experience of those who have gone before us.

Do we receive everything we need to fulfil our evangelistic calling at the moment of conversion? I don't think so. It is obvious from the New Testament that we need to be filled with the Holy Spirit and it would appear that this experience is often powerful and discernible. It may be accompanied by speaking in tongues or by a physical manifestation of the power of the Spirit. This may happen at the time of conversion and it's better if it does, given the centrality of the work of the Spirit to the Christian life. However, many don't hear about the Spirit until much later in their Christian experience and therefore often have an experience of this kind when they hear more about the Spirit and His gifts. Others reach a stage of desperation in their experience of the Christian life, having tried to live it out in their own strength. God then meets them once they come to the end of themselves and what I would take to be normative Christian experience then begins.

Having said this, I don't really have a "two stage" initiation theology ie. 1. conversion and 2. baptism in the Spirit. I believe that baptism in the Spirit is a further Pauline way of speaking about conversion, so that theologically these terms mean the same thing. However, the disciples clearly needed more than one personal encounter with the Spirit and we are told to *go on being filled with the Spirit* (Ephesians 5:18). Therefore, it seems to me that the second experience comes between the first and the third, and that we need to go on experiencing the Spirit.

There may still be some significance in an idea about the Spirit borrowed from the Old Testament. There, oil was sometimes poured out and people were said to be "anointed" with the Spirit. I believe that evangelists need to be anointed by the Spirit if this can be taken to imply a more "external" empowerment for service. Furthermore, it seems to me that we should pray that the anointing upon us might increase. Anointing carries with it the sense of effectiveness: not only am I doing what I believe I am called to do, but what I am doing is clearly bearing fruit. People who are anointed to evangelise are not only able to represent the Gospel but are also able to bring people to faith. Of course, we have to be careful here in that there are times when people do not respond – and that has nothing to do with us. I think that this anointing comes or increases when we recognise (or are forced to recognise) that we are not up to the job and then call upon God to empower us in the knowledge that if He doesn't, we've had it! The recognition of our weakness does not in itself make us effective in God's service. However, the realisation by faith of our weakness and God's strength is a powerful combination.

Therefore, the starting point for evangelists is to seek and keep on seeking the power of the Spirit. My experience has been that God wants to use people in His service who want to be used. They may not start out as His most polished representatives, but they have the desire to see God do what they know He can do – and God likes that. I know this is true because I had a tremendous desire to see God at work when I became a Christian and to get involved in the action. At a personal level, I was often insensitive, aggressive and ill-informed. I spent quite some time telling non-Christians that Jesus claimed to be the way the truth and *the light!* When an exasperated Christian friend pointed this out for the third time I still couldn't see what the problem was. Surely I was close enough? Also when I discovered preaching no one commented favourably about what I said for two years. In fact, I was pretty terrible – but this didn't stop God using me.

I love this verse:

"Give and it will be given to you. A good measure, pressed down, shaken together and running over will be poured into your lap." (Luke 6:38)

We should seek the power of the Spirit and then "give away" what we receive as we speak of Jesus. Then we should come back and ask to be empowered by the Spirit again! Of course, the process of seeking God for a particular thing will probably lead to us being changed in ways that might not seem to be directly connected. But we ourselves are the channels through which the message comes and the more Christ-like we are, the more effective we shall be at preaching the Gospel.

I don't believe that praying a lot in this way is an excuse for not using our minds or seeking to become effective as speakers. Charismatics often denigrate the mind as though it is invariably opposed to the Spirit. This has led to the phenomenon of the technically awful preacher who is nevertheless effective – though no one can quite understand how! I believe that Christ has been and will continue to renew my mind and, like Paul, I want to sing with my mind and spirit and also preach with my mind and spirit.

How do you know when you're anointed enough? That's a non-question in that we cannot measure the fullness of the Spirit and logically even the most powerfully used Christians could be more powerfully used! We have to go in the strength we have and shouldn't fall into unbiblical passivity. Before I preach or speak to non-Christians I assume I'm as filled with the Spirit as I can be right now, given that I am asking Him to fill me. It says in the Bible, *"How much more will the Father give the Holy Spirit to those who ask?"* (Luke 11:13). I assume that since I have asked, He has heard me. I've also noticed that if something more unusual is going to happen, I have a more tangible sense of the anointing of the Spirit. But often when I pray that the Spirit will be poured out on and through me, I feel nothing in particular.

The Spirit and Evangelism

Not only do we need to seek the power of the Spirit before we speak of Jesus, but we also need to become sensitive to the Spirit as we are speaking. Once, I was invited to speak at an evangelistic barbecue. Just before I was due to begin, I noticed a boy who was limping as he tried to play various sports. I asked him what had happened to his leg and he told me the details. I then asked him if he would allow me to pray that Jesus would heal him. Like many non-Christians, he was perfectly happy to be prayed for. So we went somewhere private and I told him how we wanted to pray for him (asking the Spirit to come and with the laying on of hands etc.) then I asked him to pray first.

I said, "You can pray in your head if you want." But he said, "No, it's okay – Jesus, please heal me!" That made me nervous! Perhaps not surprisingly, the Spirit came upon him and we could see his leg being moved around and he said that it felt very hot. After a few moments he got up and started doing various exercises. I was hoping this wouldn't lead to hospitalisation, being the great man of faith that I am! Anyway, God had healed him and we then went through Mark's Gospel and I showed him some of the healing accounts, explained what Jesus has done for us and then he became a Christian.

God sometimes shows me particular individuals He is working in, or conditions He wants to heal. I know that "revelations" of this kind can be quite general leading some to doubt their efficacy. I once had a revelation about four hours before a meeting I was speaking at for someone who was going on a cycling holiday to France, but who had genital problems! I regard that as fairly specific and I gave this word at the end of my talk. A young man sidled up to me just as I was leaving to say (very quietly) that it was him!

I lost my sense of embarrassment about these things some time ago now and I really don't care what I feel led to say any longer. Indeed, we have to learn to go with what we believe God is saying or doing. I've found that these specific intimations from God often open the door for a more general or increased work of the Spirit.

It isn't unusual for the anointed preaching of the Gospel to be challenged by demonised people. This was, of course, normal in the New Testament. Disquiet amongst the demonised continues to be one indicator of how much spiritual impact is being made on a given occasion. I believe that evangelists should ensure that they are trained in praying for healing and deliverance. The preaching of the Gospel, healing, and casting out of demons constituted Jesus' main activities and were included in the commission to the twelve and to the seventy (Luke9:1,10:1f). If we are more used to the former and less comfortable with the latter then we are falling short of the biblical norm. I have always felt that where my experience doesn't conform to the biblical one, then I clearly need to seek a different experience.

When we are seeking to be open to the Spirit in these ways, wonderful things can happen. When I was at theological college, a group of about 120 American students came to stay for a couple of weeks during our summer holiday. One morning when I was praying for opportunities to speak to them about Jesus, I did what I sometimes do and fell asleep. While I was sleeping I dreamt that I had a conversation with a young guy who I had never actually spoken to, but whose name I knew to be Steve. I then had another dream in which I was preaching to all the students. Being a very spiritual man, I instantly dismissed this as a flight of spiritual fancy and got on with my day.

That evening I went to join the queue for what my college called "food". Steve and a gorilla-like friend of his were addressing an eternal question: "What do girls want?" I thought I'd join in so that we could pool our profound ignorance. The gorilla indicated with great admiration that Steve was really cool because he never let girls get close to him. I think he meant emotionally. In my dream of that morning I'd said to Steve, "You've experienced something in your life which has caused you to close your emotions off to other people. If you carry on like that you're going to die inside, but Jesus wants to heal you." So when the gorilla alluded to Steve's emotional detachment, I said, "Well, that's very interesting." They said to me, "What do you mean, 'interesting'?"

I asked if I could speak to Steve on his own. The gorilla loped off. I asked Steve if he believed in God and he said, "No" in a very emphatic way. I said, "Well, you might find this difficult then, but this is what happened when I was praying this morning..."

I told him what Jesus had shown me and then asked him if it meant anything to him. He told me his story. He had never been close to his parents and had developed no close friends until a year ago when he met a girl. He fell in love with her, cried when he made love to her, and knew this was "the real thing". Sadly, she had just stolen $11,000 from him before he came to England. So he decided that he would never trust another person as long as he lived. Obviously, what God showed me spoke to him. He came to talk to me a couple of times, cried a lot and experienced the Spirit. Partly because of what happened to Steve, I was invited to preach to all the Americans. Quite a few became Christians.

I could easily have missed what the Spirit was doing and I'm quite confident that I have on other occasions. This story demonstrates that God will use anyone who is seeking to be open to Him – even people like me, who are not as good at discerning God's direction as we should be. But above all, it demonstrates the incredible compassion of God, who reached out to that young person because He wanted to heal him. It is our enormous privilege to collaborate with God as He seeks and saves the lost. In order to do so, we must be men and women of the Spirit.

8
Evangelism as Preaching

A Context For Proclamation

Once I was invited to speak at what was described as "an evangelistic youth service". About 30 or 40 *bona fide* teenagers duly trooped in, as did many others whom youth had long since deserted! The event contained all the elements of a church service – worship, prayers, a sermon, etc. – and I still struggle to think of anything less appropriate to the non-Christians present than what we endured that night. The worship was led by a man who could neither sing in tune nor play his guitar with a consistent rhythm. He insisted on explaining in great detail the "real meaning" of each and every chorus we sang. In my experience, the real meaning of most choruses is so self-explanatory that if you need an explanation you probably need quite a lot of other things as well. The "band" that accompanied him could *never* have formed a musical whole, even if all the musicians involved had been world class – which they weren't.

My talk was preceded by a time of reflection and meditation on the meaning of the cross. This turned out to be an opportunity for the service leader to make his own lengthy and awful presentation of the Gospel. The culmination of this nightmare experience was an invitation to write down a brief account of our major sins, so that we could go and attach them to a cross that he had brought with him. The cross, which was about a metre tall, wobbled a lot on its stand. It was constructed from a material which made the attachment of pieces of paper virtually impossible. Deeply fascinated, I watched as people actually participated in this game, including some teenagers ("Probably Christians!" I thought bitterly). Sadly, however, a few seconds or minutes after the paper records of people's sins had been attached to the cross, they fell off. Unbelievably, after all this had finally ended, somebody led us in prayer and his main focus was on how we needed to confess our sins – again!

I hate this kind of thing.

That night I believe I received an anointing of desperation. All else had abjectly failed. What could be done to redeem the situation in any way? This is by no means the first time I've found myself in this position and I'm quite sure that others reading this book will have plenty of horror stories of their own. You might protest, "Surely these people were only doing their best?" You might say that I'm being unloving or arrogant. In my view, the lack of loving care exhibited by these Christians who served up mindless pap to the starving was inexcusable. The arrogance in this situation was exhibited by those same Christians, when they refused to change their normal practice in any way to accommodate outsiders.

Just as most people in this country have no idea what Christianity is, most Christians in this country have no idea how to create a context in which outsiders will be comfortable. For example, when a more traditional service begins and proceeds without explanation, we demonstrate that we are performing for the faithful (who pride themselves on not needing to be reminded of such things) and have not one jot of concern for outsiders. That's like members of a wine club carrying on as normal, assuming that new members will get with the programme over time or leave. In other words, many see the local church as their club with its particular rules and practices, and if someone hangs around long enough, who knows, they might penetrate the mysteries of why they do what they do!

I mention this first because the context in which preaching or the presentation of the Gospel takes place is very important. I have led Alpha courses for about 8 years now and I'm confident that the course context is one of the main reasons why it has been so effective – especially amongst the middle classes. Alpha runs for ten weeks and was initially developed at a church in central London as a means of presenting the fundamental elements of Christian truth claims, both to those who don't believe and to those who need to understand the basics of their faith more fully. If the course is run properly, it can help many un-churched or de-churched people feel as comfortable as they can in a Christian context. In fact, when I attempt to describe the course to outsiders I say, "At some stage in our lives, most of us have questions about life and spirituality. However, it is often difficult to find a context in which we can pursue these questions. Alpha provides such a context."

Significant elements of Alpha include the way in which people are welcomed when they arrive and the system by which they get a name label. They are then taken to a particular group to join others including trained group leaders. A lot of people feel more secure when they recognise that they are participating in a confidently organised process. It is, of course, highly attractive to begin an evening of this kind with food. A clear explanation of what is going to happen during the evening and of what the course is about also helps. The opportunity to respond to what they have heard in smaller groups after each talk shows respect for what people think and suggests at least that a dialogue is possible.

The relational impact of Alpha is cumulative as people choose to come back and then get to make friends with others with whom they are beginning to share their important experiences. Because Alpha is so deeply established in the culture of the church I lead, it is normal for our people to ask all new people whether they've done Alpha yet. It is also perfectly normal for members of the church to invite people to Alpha and to ignore church altogether until they have come to faith. The Alpha context revolves around the outsider and is set up entirely for his/her benefit and is therefore a much easier context than a church service.

I believe that the only way of having a meaningful "guest service" (the typical name for a church service to which people who don't normally come will be invited) is to ask "guest questions" of everything you are planning to include. These questions boil down to, "What will they make of it and will they understand it?" We keep the music up tempo and objective and the prayers focused on the needs of the world (if we have prayers). I rarely have a reading from the Bible because I do not believe that a statement of my faith is the place to start in evangelism in our culture. The service is short and the main focus is on the presentation. Everyone in our church knows that if they bring their friends they won't be embarrassed by the context. We hold services like this the Sunday before each Alpha begins. However, I'm tending to think that guest services are less effective than, say, large Alpha suppers which act as a taster for the course itself (pun intended).

What is Appropriate Proclamation?

We have seen that there is a world of difference between the proclamations of the Gospel made by Peter at Pentecost and Paul at the acropolis. If there was an inherent spiritual power in the proclamation of the history of Israel and its fulfilment in the work of her Messiah, I would have thought that those who first preached to the Gentiles would have made this proclamation. But they didn't. Indeed there are no references to the Old Testament in the record of proclamations made to the Gentiles in the Book of Acts. The starting point, as we have seen, is with elements of the existing Gentile culture. And it is useful to begin with a true story about the culture we are in. The true story that Jesus Himself uses is the story of the Kingdom of God. This is a specific spiritual story of great significance to a spiritual people at that particular time. It is therefore a good starting point.

There is no real focus on the message of the Kingdom in proclamations of the Gospel to Gentiles in Acts. Paul certainly speaks of the Kingdom in his letters, and is fully conversant with Kingdom concepts, but he does not have the same emphasis on Kingdom language as the authors of the gospels. Far from being indicative of an unbridgeable chasm separating the theologies of Jesus and Paul, this difference really reflects the movement of the Gospel from a Jewish to a Gentile context. I have noticed when I have taught about the Kingdom that there is a certain restlessness amongst my almost exclusively Gentile audience. Kingdom language is so far removed from the thought life of the people of today. In fact, there is a general sense of distrust about "kingdoms" and, if anything, they are becoming a thing of the past. I'm not saying we shouldn't teach about the Kingdom of God in church. I am saying that Kingdom language isn't a natural starting point for evangelism in a contemporary English culture.

So, I don't think that either the Old Testament story or the message of the Kingdom are the best starting points for evangelistic proclamation. Obviously, any proclamation about Jesus needs to contain information about Him, but not as a starting point. The natural starting point for any given proclamation is one of the stories of the culture. This story then needs to be related to Jesus.

I stress this because we can't assume any knowledge about Jesus or the stories about Him. We don't have an accepted basis of spirituality from which to start – as Jesus did when He preached in Israel. The point of connection is not the New Testament but the common and particular human experience of the people we are preaching to. We can be absolutely confident that their experience will conform to life "in the flesh" in all its gory detail described in various places in the Bible. In many ways, all cultures tell the same stories – stories of human love, despair, hope and pain. But all cultures have their distinctive features and we need to be alive to them.

For instance, my central London culture has stories to tell about business and the pace of life, anonymity, loneliness, stress, multiplicity of choice and disparity between the socially empowered and the disempowered. When I preach the Gospel, I begin by rehearsing a story of the kind that people tell each other on a Friday night in the pub: "We're so busy in our lives, but we don't know exactly why we're doing what we're doing, do we? ... I'm looking for the *right* person but will I be able to commit to the *same* person forever?"

My point is that Jesus met people in the context of their lives and we must do the same. I'm not sure how useful as a starting point it is to show in detail Jesus meeting people in a totally different context 2,000 years ago.

Of course, there has to come a time when people hear about the identity of Jesus, His crucifixion and resurrection. However, I wonder how many times we have failed to persuade a truly alienated person to hang around long enough to receive the message of transformation, because we haven't really connected with them. My presupposition is that people in our culture have to come to Christ from a very long way off. Therefore, if I think many of the people I'm speaking to on a given occasion are in that position, I will seek to intrigue first before seeking to convert. I need to tickle the fish, not blow them out of the water! Even in the context of Alpha, where the talks are explicitly focused on the central elements of the Christian message, I feel an increasing need to take time to make the identification between their life experience and Jesus, as opposed to jumping straight to Jesus!

Speaking to Those Who Have Never Heard Anything

If we are to flourish as a national Church or as a series of denominations, we shall have to rediscover how to present the Gospel to those who know very little about what we believe – or nothing at all. Treating them as though they know what we're talking about, or jolly well ought to know, will lead to further alienation. I think a good presentation contains the following elements:

Identification

Always introduce yourself and give a bit of information with a view to showing why they should bother to listen to you. Who are you to tell anyone about life and spirituality? Tell them! If I'm speaking to parents about bringing up children, I want them to know I have children. If I'm speaking about marriage, I want them to know I'm married. If I'm speaking to people about life and the quest for spirituality, I want them to know that I too have an experience of life and that I have been on a quest for spirituality. If I'm talking about the possibility of faith, I identify with the reality of unbelief or doubt, having been an atheist. In our culture, it is generally true that people are agnostic (they're not sure about the existence of God) and that they are suspicious of the Church. Identify with them as fully as possible. I completely understand why people aren't sure about God and even more so why they aren't sure about the Church. Make these things explicit, because it's a normal part of pub conversation. It shows that you identify with them. In becoming a human, God in Christ identified with us – despite everything that was, and is, true of us. We must extend the same courtesy to people who do not know Him if we want them to listen.

There are some Christians who think that we shouldn't talk about ourselves, only about Jesus. It is true that we must talk about Jesus, but even as we do, we are speaking of ourselves because the language we choose and the nuances of our presentation all reflect who we are. (So do our clothes, by the way). Paul spoke about himself all the time! If Jesus lives in you then especially when you are preaching Him, His glory shines through you. The idea of a necessary separation between me and the message derives from the influence of Greek thought. In Hebraic thought, mind, body and spirit are interconnected. In Greek thought, mind or spirit and body must be separated, because things to do with the body are tainted and suspect. We ought to derive our thinking from the holistic Hebraic picture. In fact, the Gospel is best expressed through ordinary people who are prepared to be real about who they are. I sense this Greek influence behind the evangelical attitude to joke telling. Either you shouldn't or, if you have to, do it at the start to assure yourself that people are going to listen for a bit! Isn't joke telling an inauthentic rhetorical trick? If you think amusing people is inauthentic, and you think you can preach without performing, then I suppose so. In my view, if there is no rhetorical technique in your preaching, you won't be any good.

Tell a culture story

By this I don't mean, "Always tell a funny story to start with." I mean, identify a story within the culture that you want to tell and tell it. Here are some easy and obvious cultural stories:

There is the story of the hopeless quest for romantic love depicted in shows like *Ally McBeal* or *Bridget Jones' Diary*. There is the story of friendship, community as a shelter, no matter what happens, as seen in *Friends*. We could probably draw a broad distinction between universal stories and particular cultural stories. Universal stories (which most people could relate to no matter where they are) might include the search for love, the search for meaning, the search for identity or the experience of suffering and struggle. Stories more specific to our post-modern context, such as in *House of Cards,* might emphasise more the fracturing of relationships, loneliness in the quest for power. Then there is the theme of the absence of overarching meaning or purpose, and the ironic identification of meaning in celebrity or trivia. If you do well on Big Brother you become somebody – for no obvious reason.

Here are some culture story examples from a sermon I recently gave at Christmas. Many people continue to enjoy a good carol service: it's part of the seasonal festivities. To my mind, this means that when they come to a carol service, they should get exactly what they want (an opportunity to get in the "Christmas spirit" by singing well known carols), but with one or two twists in the tail. I don't see the point in seeking to incorporate worship songs or asking outsiders to sing modern carols they won't know. They've come to sing, so don't disappoint them! I can see the point in performing something musical or visual as long as it's done well and is relevant. But the main twist ought to be in the sermon, where people are not so much confronted with our Christian story as they are with their own life stories.

Carol Service Talk Transcript, 2016

"Everyone makes mistakes, don't they? Obviously, *we* don't make many mistakes, *you and I* – certainly not as many as that Doreen from accounts (did you see the state of her at last year's Christmas party?) or that Nigel who does whatever he does. What is that anyway? I've no idea. (Have you seen his bird? Didn't even know they let women like that on Tinder). I'm not sure I would even call the kind of mistakes you and I make, by comparison with epic fails like your Doreens and Nigels, *mistakes* as such – more like *temporary lapses in judgement* or maybe *things we're not proud of.* 'Mistake' is a strong word, if you're talking about the likes of you and me.

It's not like *we* elected Trump (on the record for all to see and hear as a racist, wall-building, all woman-abusing, false-dream exploiting blow-hard). It's not like we're *Americans*, is it? No, but half of us did just confuse the EU with FIFA because we're tired of being told we can't wear poppies, or not being able to work out what the third official does, or losing to Germany on penalties again and again. You probably heard that the day after the vote, the most Googled question in UK was, "What is the EU"? *FIFA, mate – it's the same thing!*

Brexit wasn't us though. It was people in the North that fancied a bit of national something waving in the face of all those Poles coming over here, turning up to work on time, working for the amount of money originally agreed, actually doing good work. Bloody Poles. And don't get me started on all those child refugees just begging for an opportunity to be trafficked. That's the French for you. Probably.

Mistakes…

- Once upon a time, someone left a gate open, enabling the Turks to destroy Constantinople
- the Austrian army killed 10,000 of its own troops
- Archduke Franz Ferdinand's driver took a wrong turn, handing him on a plate to his assassin which led to WW1 and arguably

WW2

- Napoleon believed he could invade Russia in the winter
- Hitler knew he could do better than Napoleon
- the tower of Pisa took 177 years to build but only 10 to start leaning
- the Titanic didn't have enough life boats because it was "unsinkable"
- someone at NASA taped over the original and only recording of the moon landing
- someone at Decca records turned down the Beatles on the grounds that "guitar groups are on the way out"
- 12 publishers rejected the manuscript for Harry Potter

To err is human. In fact, history is simply one long record of our errs. Some mistakes have national consequences (like Brexit) and some are likely to have intergalactic consequences (like Trump). Don't be hating on my politics now – you go your way and I'll go God's.

At a much more important level, Arsene Wenger signed both Thierry Henri (one of the greatest footballers in Premier League history) but also Ya Ya Sanogo (known unaffectionately as Sanogood). Heard of him? I didn't think so.

Some errings are literally hilarious. Not *damn you* but *thank you so much*, autocorrect, for giving us so many priceless (but in this context, unrepeatable) moments of mistake-gold. Thank goodness for all the catastrophically wrong emails sent to our bosses or family members. For the apparently endless inappropriate pooh or sexual *in flagrante* discovery stories. Where would we be without these? Quite possibly, doing the work that is actually being done by the Poles.

Some mistakes are really painful. They can't be laughed off and they don't have a happy ending. Like me missing the last time my mother was conscious enough to say goodbye before she died. Me getting engaged to the wrong person. Me not sorting things out with my brother before he took his own life…

Which raises the question: *what do we do with our mistakes?...*"

Tell the Jesus Story

Once we have told a culture story, we are in a position to speak about Jesus, which is, of course, what we really want to do. In a way, I was encouraged when one man who had never been to church told me after I gave a sermon similar to the one above that he could relate to what I was saying, "Until the Jesus bit"! If you assume he's coming from miles and miles away, this is a good start.

In so far as we can, we need to express the story in contemporary language and idiom and in order to do this we are going to need to be in touch with popular thought. I still listen avidly to contemporary music, paying particular attention to any acts that are really popular. The same applies to film, TV and adverts. The really popular ones have obviously caught onto something in terms of image or lyrics, for instance, that expresses a culture story. We also need to know where the debate about Jesus currently stands. This will be very much affected by the values of a particular culture, since all cultures seek to recast Jesus in their own image. For instance, in the 60s, Jesus was seen as a revolutionary figure. In ours, He might be seen as the champion of non-judgementalism.

Having told a culture story, we need to connect it with Jesus, who He is and what He says, with a view to encouraging people to take their enquiries further. Here is how I continued on in my Carol service sermon:

"...*What do we do with our mistakes?* Do you know what I do? I talk to Jesus.

Oh, that's nice ... for him ... isn't it? He talks to Jesus.

Gentle Jesus, meek and mild. Ah, bless. He probably has an elf friend and a pet unicorn, too. He's all religious, isn't he? I wish I had his faith, but I can't be religious though, can you? No, certainly not. Why not? Science ... suffering ... sausages. It's all been disproved, hasn't it? A sky-scraper fitting into a thimble, a battleship into your pocket, God into a baby? Come on, you're having a laugh. Anyway, think about the expression: "virgin birth". Virgin and birth just don't go together, do they? Like ice-cream and bacon. And why didn't God write it in the sky then, if He exists? Granted there were angels in the sky and a star in the sky, but *He could have written it in the sky, couldn't He?*

And why didn't He let anyone know it was going to happen? It's not like He told anyone what He was going to do so they could understand, was it? Granted there was your Isaiah and your Jeremiah and your David and your whole people of Israel who knew a Messiah would come. And there was your Anna and your Zechariah and your Mary and your Joseph and your wise men and your shepherds and your sheep. But it wasn't like anyone foretold it, did they, or there were your actual witnesses, were there?

And why is the whole thing so upside down? Why wasn't the baby the product of a one-night stand between your Brangelinas and your Beckhams so we could follow the whole thing in *Hello*? Why wasn't a Royal involved and a palace and an army? Why was it *so tenuous* that there wasn't even room in an inn for the pregnant woman, so she has to give birth in a stable, putting the baby in a feeding trough with the stench of manure all around? How can something so humble, so unassuming, so apparently touch-and-go possibly be God? If God really wanted to reveal Himself why didn't He wait until now? He could tweet it, post it or Snapchat it. Then we'd believe, because we all believe everything we see on social media, don't we?

Surely this service with its pretty little candles, and its reminiscence of childhood nostalgia, and its vaguely familiar churchiness must be a mistake – or at least those who believe it must be mistaken, right?

Jesus of Nazareth goes on to live a life devoid of material comfort. He has neither a home nor public office. He never writes a book. He does none of the things we would normally associate with greatness. He spends a large amount of His time with the modern equivalent of paedophiles, crack whores, phone-hackers and thieves – those who have long since stopped trying to hide the mistakes of life. He also spends time with the religious who refuse to admit the mistakes of their lives because they still have a reputation to maintain.

And to everyone He proclaims the importance of a life of seemingly impossible standards: turn the other cheek (no anger), do not commit adultery (no lust), do not kill (no hate), love your enemy (no selfishness), do good things to those who treat you badly (no grudges). And this led to the inevitable question: *who could ever live a life like that?* And to the inevitable answer: not one of us with our history of and propensity for mistakes. But Jesus uniquely walks the talk and lives the most beautiful life we have ever seen. Oh, and He also heals the sick, feeds the hungry, calms the storm, restores the lost and raises the dead, to show us what a human being made in the image of God, but without mistakes, can really do. And yet, unlike the religious, He doesn't distance Himself from mistakes and their consequences. He throws Himself into them. The most important thing Christianity says about God is that He doesn't turn away from us at our point of greatest failure; He turns towards us in it, beginning with an act in which, indeed, a skyscraper fits itself into a thimble, in which Almighty God clothes Himself with the frail flesh of a baby.

Notice that when the baby grows up, all the armies that ever marched, all the navies that ever sailed, all the kings and queens that ever reigned, have not affected our life on earth as much as that one solitary life. Is it not worth considering the claims of a person of this magnitude?

Experience says that we are interested in the big questions of life; questions like, *does life have a meaning? Is there a God and what happens when we die?* But we lack a context in which to explore these questions properly, other than down the pub when we answer all the questions, but then can't remember what we concluded the next day. So we run a course called the *Life Course* for those who have questions about life and its meaning. The next one begins on ... Each evening there is great food and the team brings wine. There is a stimulating presentation and an opportunity for small group discussion. People choose whether they want to be in a discussion group to explore the big questions or whether they are doing the course to integrate into the church. Obviously the small group discussion is appropriate to the make-up of the group. The presentations start right at the beginning with a consideration of the question, *what gives meaning to our lives?* And we go on from there. We do present Christian claims, but aim to create an open debate in which anyone can discuss anything. Anyone is welcome to come. If you come once and decide not to return, no one comes hunting you down. We are not interested in your money and we aren't trying to induct you into our cult! Talk to me afterwards if you think this might be interesting or pick up a brochure on your way out. Thanks for listening."

Tell Them How to Take Things Further

If I'm speaking to those who have heard very little or nothing before, then I challenge them to take their enquiries further. I might say something like this:

"If you have been interested by what you've heard and would like a context in which to explore things a bit more, can I recommend a course we run in the church called Alpha? It's a 10 week course that runs on Wednesday evenings. We begin with highly edible food which is served from 7.00pm until 7.45. You don't have to eat with us if you don't want to. At 7.50 there's a short account of how somebody came to faith and then usually I speak for about 30 minutes. Then we get some coffee (which is essential by this stage) and we go into small groups where there is an opportunity to discuss what we've heard, state any opinions or objections or just listen to the discussion. It doesn't matter if you don't feel you know very much; this is a context for those who want to explore the questions that we all have with like-minded people, not a Bible class.

If you can't come every week it doesn't matter – just come as much as you want. In fact, you can come once and if you don't like it, you don't have to come back. No one will come hunting you down. We're not interested in your money and if you eat the food, I promise that you won't end up drugged and imprisoned in a squat in Cricklewood!"

If people want to hear more about Jesus and are willing to come to an Alpha course, for example, I think it's very important that we are able to defend intelligently the main things that we believe. Preachers of the Gospel must study and continue to study the very best ways of presenting and explaining the fundamental claims which are that Jesus is the Son of God, that He died for our sins, and that He has been raised from the dead. I especially enjoy contrasting the claims of Jesus with those of other religious leaders and presenting a detailed case from a lawyer's perspective of the evidence for the resurrection. I have also worked very hard to find the best ways I can of explaining concepts such as sin or the meaning of Jesus' death.

Those who see the apologetic imperative as a denial of confidence in the "simple message of the Gospel" haven't noticed how radically the simple message changes in different contexts. Neither have they noticed just how much Paul engages his not inconsiderable brain in the process of preaching and teaching. If you are dealing with people who don't know anything, it is obvious that they are going to need to be convinced. You cannot convince people about the coherence of what you believe unless you know how and why it coheres! This requires work, but what else would evangelists want to do with their lives?

9
Evangelism in the Real World

Back to the beginning. I think we all know that it isn't pretty out there. There may be nostril-frothing revival in other parts of the world, but here we are in the grip of what appears to be a remorseless decline in Church membership and a corresponding retreat into godlessness in the country. As I have already so unkindly stated, I believe that this is largely our fault! When the Church ceases to express the dynamic life of the Spirit, the people of the Church fail to live as the people of God. When the people of God cease to be true to their calling, the people of the land (like sheep without a shepherd) wander off in any number of senseless and inane sheep-like directions. We know that the Bible sometimes likens us to lost sheep and when it does, it is never a compliment! Sheep are profoundly stupid animals who will, for example, continue to gather in their chosen part of a field, even if it is the only part of the field where there is a snowdrift. Also, once sheep have turned over onto their backs for whatever reason, they are incapable of getting up! We all know that they specialise in wandering off and getting lost. They need shepherds and, if there are no shepherds, then sheep are in danger of making poor life choices.

It is well known that whenever the people of the land cease to trust in God they do not come to believe in *nothing*, but in *anything* and the result is widespread darkness. The movement towards darkness has been greatly assisted over recent decades by the unravelling of any communal or shared ethical fabric that once held us together. Our culture's affirmation of the pursuit of unrestrained personal autonomy leaves more and more of us sitting all alone in our rooms, where we are at our most dangerous! Since I've been a Christian, things have definitely got darker (I *think* that's a coincidence), but I suggested in chapter two that we might adopt the attitude that since the darkest time is always just before the dawn, this must be a great time to be alive. The history of our country with its great spiritual awakenings suggests that Jesus will surely return to us in all His power and many are praying that we shall see widespread transformation across the country once again.

In the meantime, we should take heart from our personal experience of preaching the Gospel, which continues to demonstrate that God's arm is not too short to save. Of course, we dream of the kind of empowering that will lead to revival, but we mustn't fall into the trap of thinking that ours is a passive role in which we are simply to pray and wait for God to act in a new way. It seems to me that God doesn't generally "God" people, but prefers instead to do His work in some kind of partnership with us, both in prayer and in evangelism. So we must go in the strength we have with the message of the Gospel. We are called to preach the Gospel in and out of season, not to sit around waiting for the heady days of spiritual summer.

Furthermore, it is arguable that God has already visited His Church over the last 30 or 40 years with His renewing power. Our task (which we do not seem to have come to terms with) is to work out how to move from the blessed confines of a renewal meeting and on into the world, taking with us the power we so often receive at those meetings. I wonder how much power has slowly ebbed away from our lives simply because it hasn't been given away through ministry and witness.

Of course, it may be that our situation is not what it seems, because God's ways and perspective bear so little relation to ours. For instance, He is attracted to human weakness and therefore He is almost certainly drawn to our plight, characterised as it is by moral and spiritual bankruptcy. The very powerlessness of our situation is probably calling forth from the compassionate heart of God a desire to visit us in power once again. He knows how useless we are and remembers with kindness the fact that we are dust! However, according to the Bible, He does seem to look for people who are aware of the poverty of their present experience and are willing to lament about it.

Once again, the story of Gideon comes to mind. In Judges 6:1f we learn that the people of Israel are oppressed by the Midianites who are making vicious use of that ancient weapon of mass destruction – the camel. Gideon's protests about the plight of his nation draw a surprising response from God: *"The Lord is with you mighty warrior"* (6:12). It seems as though the Holy Spirit inspires in us this kind of lamentation of our plight and it becomes a prelude to the demonstration of God's might.

But we should always be ready to go in the strength we have, particularly when it doesn't appear to be very much. We need to have the courage to give away the little we have so that God can increase the measure (Luke 6:38). We should be encouraged by the fact that a good evangelist is a bad evangelist that got better, someone who has *learnt* to give away the little he/she has. Effective evangelists *learn* to function where they are with the resources they have. They *learn* to be faithful with whatever God has entrusted to them and usually start small. There is a lot of learning involved! So as we come to the end of this book, it might be worth reflecting on our personal world. Where are we today in our life situation, our relationship with

God, our experience of the Spirit and of evangelism? What is God teaching us at the moment?

Let me introduce you to an ideal world in which there are found perfect answers to these questions. In an ideal world, the communication of our faith in Jesus would be a natural feature of our everyday lives. Indeed, we would develop a pattern of life that is so radical in its conformity to the pattern of Jesus that it would demand an explanation. And we would be only too happy to explain! In an ideal world, we would begin the Christian life with an encounter of such transforming power that our struggle would be to keep from screaming with delight about our faith – as opposed to struggling to keep our "credibility" now that we're lumbered with believing in God.

In an ideal world, we would also develop a clear evangelistic strategy. Oh yes, we would strategize and take a long-term view about the communication of our faith, realising that with some we are there for the long haul and that with many, many others we shall be merely a link (though an essential link) in a long chain leading to conversion. And those closest to us, who deserve our most careful consideration, would get it. After all, they have put up with us all these years and therefore we would try to honour the integrity of our existing relationships, having come to faith. I hope that you will do what I say in this instance and not what I did! Sadly, I simply ditched those from amongst my friends who weren't interested in Christianity.

Because our lives have become intertwined with theirs, those closest to us will have particular concerns and questions about our conversion. Like, how will this affect our sex-life/living arrangements, marriage, working practices, the dynamics of our friendship or parent-child relationship or the things we spend our time doing together? My parents had me surreptitiously checked out by a doctor when I became a Christian. Not before time you might say! We need to give people space to explore these questions with us and we may not always know the answer straight away. When you think about it, it isn't surprising that the reality of our conversion can send seismic shock waves through our friends and relations, because the dynamics of our lives (and by implication the dynamics of theirs) are being changed. People like change as much as they like trips to the hospital for major surgery. Not every violent reaction to our conversion is the result of demonic opposition. Most are borne out of human fear.

In an ideal world, we would seek to win over or reassure those closest to us by the way in which we live out our faith, so that they might see a real and positive change in us. A man and his wife once reached an apparently petty, yet incredibly real impasse in their relationship. It focused on the vexed question of who ought to be responsible for emptying the kitchen rubbish bin. In the wife's family, the tradition was that this was the man's job, whilst the opposite was true in the husband's family. Neither was willing to compromise. The husband became a Christian and began to feel that God was asking him to take out the rubbish. Only when he began to do so did the wife realise that something significant had happened to her husband. She became a Christian thereafter.

In an ideal world, we would be perfectly capable of answering the intellectual questions that our friends have and, even more amazingly, we would have the wisdom to know when to stop talking as well! We would manage to cope with derision and misunderstanding, continuing to seek to love and spend time with those who despise our faith in Jesus. We would also maintain that fine balance between being with people who continue to say and do things that aren't right and becoming judgemental, feeling threatened or even envious and compromising ourselves. In an ideal world, we would know where to take those we love to hear the Gospel stated more directly than our relationship will currently allow. In an ideal world, we would have an openness to the Spirit when talking about God and also the boldness to take the opportunities He so often presents when we are looking for them.

I'm sure that most of us have experienced the ideal to one degree or another. Some have a remarkable conversion story. Some have already seen friends and family come to faith because of what has happened to them and many have made radical decisions about lifestyle as a result of conversion. But none of us lives in an ideal world. Some come slowly and gradually to faith. Most make serious mistakes in what they've said and done along the way and some will know the pain of having compromised the integrity of their witness with people close to them.

Now some sermons (and I'm sure books) about evangelism merely serve to emphasise the painful gap between what we might be doing and what we are actually doing, as though a good dose of guilt will sort us out! Sermons on giving and prayer also seem to lend themselves to this treatment. But I learnt a long time ago that guilt is only useful if it drives us to the cross and is useless if it drives our other behaviour. We shouldn't evangelise because we'd feel guilty if we didn't!

So let's have look at the real world and seek to start there.

In the Real World, We Aren't All Evangelists

It is a gift of the Spirit to bring people to faith in Jesus and to be effective in the way we speak about Him to people who don't believe. Not everyone has this gift. There are different kinds of evangelist, but "real ones" often have common tendencies as I have suggested in chapter four. This is exaggerated, but we are often drama queens, given to hyperbole and the sound of our own voices. We flit from person to person loving the challenge of the new. We are passionate about anything that interests us and can probably make a debate about wallpaper sound compelling if necessary. It doesn't matter to us that much if people don't agree with what we're saying in the sense that it doesn't usually threaten our faith. We're usually more convinced than most! We may not be that motivated by people unless we're converting or counting them. We are motivated by the overall mission to proclaim the Gospel and by convincing people about Jesus.

Thank God, though, that not everyone is like this! If you have read this book and you have come to the conclusion that you really aren't an evangelist, I wouldn't try to become one. Instead, I would aim to be a *witness* – someone who points to Jesus by the way they are and by what they say. Evangelists enjoy a privileged life because they so often witness the moment of conversion. However, I am profoundly aware that though some have needed me to announce the message at a particular time, they have needed far more their Christian friends and family, the faithful witnesses who have pointed them to Christ and have prayed for them, sometimes throughout their lives. People who join living churches so often seem to be consciously aware of the presence of God amongst us, but that has far more to do with the power of our Spirit-filled lives when we gather together in one place than with what is said at the front. Therefore, even if you don't consider yourself to be an evangelist, it would be good to have a vision for becoming an effective witness.

If you are an evangelist, it is good to have a vision for becoming as effective as possible and I hope that some of the issues raised in this book will stimulate you to further growth in your gift. When I was at theological college, I did a placement in the East End of London with an incredible man called John Pearce. He said something that has always stayed with me and it was this: "Consider the possibility of becoming a *great* preacher." Now, I have not become a great preacher, but I am at least a better preacher than I was and have sometimes felt spurred on by the challenge he gave me as a young man. So all evangelists should consider the possibility of becoming *great* evangelists! It is good to aim high.

In the Real World, Young Christians Combine Maximum Opportunity with Minimum Maturity

Typically, this is the time when we are in relationship with a whole group of people untouched by the Gospel, who we can surely influence for Christ. And yet at this very time, we are sadly lacking in basic knowledge, spiritual wisdom, a consistent lifestyle, faith and sensitivity. Our only real weapons are 1. *enthusiasm* – not to be underestimated and 2. we may be particularly *filled with the Spirit* – also not to be underestimated.

This is, of course, so typical of God who uses the weak things of the world to shame the strong. Doesn't make it any less frustrating though! It has taken me years to learn when to speak and when not to speak. It has taken me years to learn how to communicate publicly and privately with those who don't believe. I'm sure that there are naturals in this, as in anything else, but I surely have not been one of them. And yet I believe that God called me from my first days of faith to preach the Gospel. He showed me that passage in Genesis where Abraham was told that his descendants would be as numerous as the stars (Genesis 15:5f). I really have no idea how many have been converted through me, but I do know that I have made some spectacular mistakes. Once, I got talking to the sister of the bride at a wedding reception and after a while she began to cry. The top table became very concerned and there was some suspicion that I might have been trying to strike up an inappropriate relationship! Actually,

I allowed the intensity of the conversation to mount on what was already a very emotional day for her. I should have changed the subject earlier. You live and learn!

In the Real World, Mature Christians Often Have Other Things to Think About

Maturity in the faith and in our human development tend to go together and maturity emerges through experience and therefore comes with age. But other things come with age too, like responsibilities of many kinds. We often come to envy the passion of the new convert, but have got too many things to think about to just drop everything and follow the direction of the Spirit – even for a day. We have busy jobs and busy lives and the euphoria of our conversion experience can feel as though it is being slowly dissipated by the concerns of the daily grind. We are definitely in church and can be relied upon to be there, but in practice we have come to leave the mission of the church to other people. In practice, our lives really become focused around our jobs and the needs of our children.

So, in the real world not everyone is an evangelist, though we are all witnesses. New converts lack some of what it takes to be truly effective in evangelism, except the impetus to evangelise, and mature converts who have a lot more of what it takes often seem to lack the impetus. It doesn't have to be like this – *but in the real world, it often is.* And this is probably at least partly why the Church doesn't grow as it might. So I've tried to think about three distinctive marks of an effective evangelistic lifestyle as a way of concluding and summarising this book. I'm going to refer to the account of the meeting between Philip and the Ethiopian eunuch (Acts 8:26f) in order to do so.

1. Openness to the Spirit's power (v26,29,39)

This isn't your average, everyday story of personal evangelism. Phillip has been conducting a very successful mission when the Spirit speaks to him and directs him to do something very unusual: leave what is really a revival and head off into the desert. Accounts such as this are selected because they are so stunning. I do the same in my much smaller way on Alpha. If I want to talk about healing, I will probably choose a significant example and one that is more difficult to explain other than in terms of God. Therefore, it will be (by the standards of my experience) in the more dramatic category. This remarkable act of obedience on Phillip's part leads to the conversion of a very important man who comes from a region which has yet to receive the Gospel.

However dramatic or otherwise are our experiences of the Spirit when we evangelise, there is no doubt from the New Testament that there is a direct connection between effective evangelism and the power of the Spirit as we have seen in chapter seven. Evangelism isn't something we do *to* people – it is something we do *for* people under the inspiration of the Spirit. As I have written, there have been times when I have "known" by the power of the Spirit that quite large numbers of people at a given event will make a commitment to Jesus when the time comes to do so. I interpret this "knowing" as a special gift of God, by which He lets me in on the action! He tells me what He is doing. I wish it happened all the time, but it simply doesn't. I have learnt that when that particular confidence comes upon me it is a response to what the Spirit is doing and that I am being equipped to play my part.

But, if for whatever reason, the Spirit is not working in that way, I cannot make it happen. If an elephant is walking down a narrow jungle path and you encounter him, it is infinitely easier to turn round and head in the same direction as the oncoming beast than to try and squeeze past him. In the same way, if the Spirit is moving in a particular direction, it is much easier to seek to follow Him than to stick with determination to our own agenda. The trick is obviously to grow in our ability to discern what the Spirit is doing. I find that I go through times when I am more and less filled with the Spirit and therefore experience varying degrees of sensitivity to His voice. Having to get myself into a place of receptivity helps. For instance, if I am speaking or leading and will need to know what the Spirit is doing. So does the growing awareness that I have gradually become less open to the Spirit. It is at these times that the lamentation begins which leads to renewal, etc. But I know that if I want to be effective, I must maintain a listening heart towards the Spirit and seek to do what He is doing.

2. Ability to answer questions (v32-35)

There is no getting away from it: Phillip knows the answers to this man's questions. He is comfortable with the Old Testament and can interpret this passage from Isaiah in the light of Jesus. He understands what the eunuch is reading. My recollection of initial conversations with Christians at university was that they didn't know as much as I did, especially about religion! It is essential that evangelists are able to convince people about the reliability of our faith claims. Being well informed about why we believe what we believe is a fundamental prerequisite to effective evangelism. It isn't surprising that some Christians don't feel that confident when they try to explain what they believe. They don't really know! It may feel like doing a ten week course about plumbing, of which you missed weeks four and seven, and then being asked to deal with a plumbing situation that requires knowledge imparted on the weeks when you weren't there!

Many of us have been extremely well educated and yet we often seem to be content with a vague understanding of the faith that we affirm to be essential to our very existence. This seems strange to me. In fact, we need to grow in our intellectual understanding of God, just as we need to grow in our experience of Him. There is also a lot to be said for understanding some of the major philosophical presuppositions that underlie people's questions about the faith. For instance, questions about the uniqueness of Jesus, the co-equal viability of all spiritualities, or ethical frameworks that presuppose there is no such thing as absolute truth. In other words, most people in England today are confirmed relativists, even if they are unfamiliar with the label. It is worth exploring the dimensions of relativism, since many contemporary questions have relativist presuppositions at their foundation.

3. Openness to people (v27-31)

Effective evangelists have the ability to relate naturally to people who don't yet believe. I could say they know how to respect other people's personal and intellectual boundaries. In this very unusual situation, Phillip makes a very good approach. He is direct without being aggressive or offensive. 90% of effective evangelism is love and one way of showing love is to respect other people's boundaries. In other words, if they don't want to know, don't force them. Many of those who had been following Jesus left Him after His teaching about the necessity of feeding on Him to find life (John 6:25f). We don't read of Jesus chasing after them down the road, imploring them to come back.

We need to feed people according to what they can take at any given time. If I want to feed a baby, I don't toss it chicken leg. I peel off the skin, cook the meat, put it in a liquidiser and then use a spoon. Being sensitive to whether people have heard enough at any moment is difficult – especially when we are trying to persuade them – but it is essential. If possible, I tend to avoid winning the argument these days. I prefer to seek to help people to convince themselves. Sometimes we become confused and it's almost as if it's our reputation that we're worrying about when we're in the middle of a debate. But, of course, it is God's Gospel and He is able to defend His own reputation. Some find elements of Christian teaching very hard to take. The thing is though, that it isn't our teaching it's God's and the ultimate struggle people are having is not with us but with Him. Let's not take someone's struggle with God personally! It is encouraging to bear in mind that some of the staunchest adversaries of the Gospel eventually signed up. In so far as we can, we need to be the kind of people they will return to when the Spirit has finally broken through to them and convicted them of the truth.

I believe that at the moment the stakes are high. We cannot allow the trend towards spiritual decline to continue for the sake of all those who are living and dying without the hope of Christ. There is no point in disregarding church, although formal church in this country has largely failed. The re-emergence of true church, energised and directed by the Spirit as a living sign of the power of the Gospel is the only hope our country has. Clearly we need to do church wholly differently and I (together many others) am longing for the emergence of churches without walls which exist for the benefit of our alienated culture.

Where are you right now in your real world? Are you a young Christian or have you been around for a while now? Is there a need to rediscover the freshness of the life of faith by becoming more open to the Spirit, growing in intellectual understanding or creating more space for people who don't believe?

None of us has everything together in our lives. None of us live in an ideal world. We live in the real world where there are all manner of tensions and contradictions. But we know that the real world was good enough for God, who loved it so much that He sent His Son. He is used to meeting us where we are and, in fact, He cannot meet us anywhere else. He is willing and able to take us on from there. He loves to enter into partnership with weak and broken people, so that the world might discover His glory in the face of Christ – to which the only proper response is, "Thanks be to God."

About the Author

John and Jenny Peters lead St Mary, Bryanston Square, an Anglican church in central London, where John is the Rector. Over the years the church has grown as John and others have sought to communicate the Gospel in a culturally relevant way. St Mary's has also planted several churches in the UK and abroad with similar vision and values.